# God's Message for a Growing Church

## Bob Russell

STANDARD PUBLISHING
Cincinnati, Ohio                    18-03195

Sharing the thoughts of his own heart, the author may express views
not entirely consistent with those of the publisher.

The article, "Lady in 415," is used by permission, Campus Life
Magazine, Christianity Today, Inc. Copyright © 1976.

Unless otherwise indicated, all Scripture quotations are from the
HOLY BIBLE: NEW INTERNATIONAL VERSION, Copyright © 1973,
1978, 1984 International Bible Society. Used by permission of
Zondervan Bible Publishers.

Scripture quotations from the Living Bible are copyright © 1971 by
Tyndale House Publishers. Used by permission.

**Library of Congress Cataloging-in-Publication Data**

Russell, Bob, 1943-
    God's message for a growing church / Bob Russell
        p. cm.
    ISBN 0-87403-665-8
    1. Bible. N.T. Titus--Sermons. 2. Christian Churches and
Churches of Christ--Sermons. 3. Sermons, American. I. Title.
BS2755.4.R87 1990
252'.0663--dc20                                    90-34380
                                                   CIP

to my wife, Judy,
and sons, Rusty and Phil,
whose daily support, encouragement, and prayers
have made my ministry to a growing church
a joy

# Contents

# Stand Firm in the Truth

## Titus 1:1-4

SOMEONE RECENTLY MAILED me a chart he found in a religious magazine. The chart was entitled, "The 500 Fastest Growing Churches in America." It listed the churches in the United States that had experienced the biggest numerical increase during 1987. Of the 500 churches listed of every denomination possible, Southeast Christian Church in Louisville, Kentucky was listed as sixth in the nation. Our worship attendance had increased by over 1200 people in one year.

That statistic both thrills me and frightens me. It thrills me because anybody would want to be a part of something that dynamic. But I have to be careful that those numbers don't become an ego thing for me. My first reaction when I saw that list was to wonder who those other five churches ahead of us were. I wondered if they were honest with their figures! But that reaction was in the wrong spirit, because we're not in competition with anybody. Our task is to sow the seed of the gospel, water it, and rejoice with whatever increase God may give.

But those figures frighten me too. How committed are those 1200 new people? How receptive are our older members? Do our people really know what they believe?

How do we utilize everybody's gifts? How can we shepherd this increasing number of people? Those are important questions to anybody who takes the church seriously.

That's the reason for this study of Paul's letter to Titus. Paul had started a church on the island of Crete. It was on the grow. Paul put Titus in charge of overseeing this church. He wrote Titus a letter giving instructions on how to set the church in order during its growth period. If we study it carefully, we'll learn some basics about what God wants for His church.

In his introductory remarks, Paul speaks about the importance of standing firm for the truth. In his very opening statement, Paul urges a solid commitment to a knowledge of the truth that comes from God, who does not lie. The church's primary mission is to spread abroad the truth about Jesus Christ. But probably the foremost temptation of the church is to dilute the message of the church to accommodate its culture.

## The Source of Truth

Paul begins his letter with, "Paul, a servant of God and an apostle of Jesus Christ." Jesus is the source and standard of truth. Our country right now is divided over all kinds of moral issues—pornography, the lottery, abortion, divorce, prayer in school, homosexuality, drunk driving. Dozens of moral issues have us confused because we do not know how to determine what is right and what is wrong.

Some philosophers say, "What is right is what you feel *good* after. What is wrong is what you feel *bad* after." But is that it? Should we just let people do what they feel like doing? Some people feel good only when they're stoned.

Or should we just let intelligent people or famous people in our society set the standard for right and wrong? The problem is that those people contradict each other. Who do you listen to, Jane Fonda or Phyllis Schlafly? Do you listen to Ronald Reagan or Ted Kennedy?

Maybe we ought to just let majority opinion rule. We could vote on abortion and vote on prayer in school and let the majority rule. But the problem with that is, the majority of people favored Hitler in Germany prior to World War II. The majority of the confederate states were in favor of slavery. The Bible says, "There's a way that seems right unto man, the end thereof are the ways of death."

Since there's no recognized standard of morality in our society, our culture's as confused as a termite in a yo-yo about what is right and what is wrong. But being a Christian means that you have a definite source of truth that does not change. It's not feeling and it's not majority opinion; it is the person of Jesus Christ.

When Jesus stood on trial for His life, Pilate, the governor, asked Him, "Are you the king of the Jews?"

Jesus responded, "You are right in saying I am a king. In fact, for this reason I was born, and for this I came into the world, to testify to the truth. Everyone on the side of truth listens to me."

Pilate sneered, "What is truth?" (John 18:33, 37)

But Jesus had already said, "If you're interested in the truth, you listen to me. I'm telling you the truth."

Jesus told us the truth about God. The evolutionists suggest that we are just here by accident, the result of millions of years of evolutionary changes, but Jesus said, "Have you not read that at the beginning God made them male and female?" This is the truth. You're here because of a creator.

Jesus told us the truth about man, too. The humanist says that man is getting better and better. Man eventually will solve all of his own problems, but Jesus told us the truth. "Unless you repent, you too will all perish," He said. (Luke 3:13). "I tell you the truth, everyone who sins is a slave to sin" (John 8:34).

Jesus told us the truth about himself, too. The unbeliever will condescendingly admit that Jesus was a good man and a great teacher like Muhammad or Confucius or Buddha. But Jesus told us the truth, He is God in the flesh. "I tell you the truth," He said, "before Abraham was born, I am!" (John 8:58). Though Abraham lived 2,000 years before Jesus said this, He was telling the truth. He existed before Abraham.

Jesus said, "Anyone who has seen me has seen the Father" (John 14:9). He said He came to seek and to save those that are lost, and give His life as a ransom for many. Jesus said, "I am the way and the truth and the life. No one comes to the Father except through me" (John 14:6).

Jesus told us the truth about the Bible, too. Liberals ridicule the Bible, insisting it's full of myths and contradictions. But Jesus said, "Heaven and earth will pass away, but my words will never pass away" (Matthew 24:35). In John 17:17 He prayed, "Sanctify them by the truth; your word is truth."

Jesus told us the truth about judgment, too. Universalists insist that it doesn't matter what you believe or how you behave because everybody is going to be saved eventually anyway. But Jesus said, "A time is coming when all who are in their grave will hear [my] voice and come out—those who have done good will rise to live, and those who have done evil will rise to be condemned" (John 5:28, 29).

Jesus didn't just claim to be the truth. He proved it by coming back from the grave. Anybody can go around pontificating about God and the Bible and humanity, but Jesus did more than just teach. He proved His claims by coming back after He died. He said, "As Jonah was three days and three nights in the belly of a huge fish, so the Son of Man will be three days and three nights in the heart of the earth" (Matthew 12:40). When Jesus came back to life, it vindicated His claims, it proved His deity. "God . . . commands all people everywhere to repent. For he has set a day when he will judge the world with justice by the man he has appointed. He has given proof of this to all men by raising him from the dead" (Acts 17:30, 31).

Islam is one of the fastest growing religions in the world today. Dr. Harry Rimmer tells about a discussion he had with a Muslim teacher, comparing Christianity with Islam. He said, "We believe that God created the world."

The Muslim said, "We believe God created the world."

"We believe that God has spoken to us in a book, the Bible."

"We believe God has spoken to us in a book, the Koran."

"We believe that God has visited this planet in the person of Jesus Christ."

"We believe God has revealed himself in the prophet, Muhammad."

"We believe Jesus Christ died for His people."

"We believe that Muhammad died for his people."

Dr. Rimmer said, "But we believe that Jesus Christ proved His claim by coming back from the grave."

The Muslim leader could only sadly say, "We have no record of our prophet after his death."

That is the distinctive feature about Christianity. If you go to the tomb of every other great world leader you will read the inscription, "Here he lies." But if you go to the tomb of Jesus Christ, it's empty. The words of the angel are still ringing in our ears, "He is not here; he has risen, just as he said he would" (Matthew 28:6). He told you the truth.

My hope is built on nothing less
Than Jesus blood and righteousness;
I dare not trust the sweetest frame,
But wholly lean on Jesus' name.
On Christ, the solid Rock, I stand;
All other ground is sinking sand,
All other ground is sinking sand.

## The Importance of Truth

Paul emphasizes the connection between truth and a meaningful life. In verse one it says, "Paul, a servant of God and an apostle of Jesus Christ." The truth gives you a purpose in life.

The most frequently asked question of high school graduates being interviewed for a job today is, "What goal have you set for yourself and how do you plan to achieve it?" A lot of older people couldn't answer that question, but Paul could. His goal was to be an apostle, a representative of Jesus Christ, and he was going to achieve that goal by being the Lord's servant and doing whatever the Lord wanted him to do. Once you've fully committed yourself to the truth, you have a distinct purpose. We used to sing a song in camp—"I know where I'm going and I know who's going with me."

Paul also speaks of the knowledge of the truth that leads to godliness. God's truth enhances our character. Ignorance of the truth leads to decadence, but knowledge of the truth leads to God-likeness, an improved character, integrity, self-discipline, and order.

Many were shocked at the news of a Satanic cult near Brownsville, Texas that tortured and murdered 13 young people. The parents of a University of Texas medical student who was a victim of that Satanic cult were interviewed on television. "Those people must have been possessed by the devil," the parents said. "But we need to pray for them."

Which of those two would you prefer to be your neighbor, the Satanic cult or the Christian parents who said, "We need to pray for them"? Which of those two extremes are going to make a stable society? We're not just talking about the people who go to church and the people who don't. We're talking about the very character that makes a nation strong and life meaningful. Jesus said, "The thief comes only to kill and destroy; I have come that they may have life, and have it to the full" (John 10:10).

Paul speaks of a faith and a knowledge resting on the hope of eternal life, which God, who does not lie, promised. So the truth provides hope for eternity.

Stephen Brown wrote a book entitled *When Your Rope Breaks*. Haven't you always heard, "When you get to the end of your rope, tie a knot and hold on"? What if you tie a knot and hold on and your rope breaks? You might feel your situation is that desperate. Your finances are falling apart, or your family is dissolving, or your health is broken; maybe you're addicted to a habit and you don't know whether you can break it. That kind of hopeless circumstance sometimes leads to the most extreme behavior. But the truth of Jesus Christ is that He promises the hope of eternal life even when your rope breaks.

Donna Vest is 33 years of age and has a vibrant personality. She was voted Employee of the Year at Norton's Hospital in Louisville. Some time ago she experienced headaches during a meeting and asked to be excused. Within hours she was completely paralyzed from the neck down, the result of a rare disease involving a blood clot at the base of the brain. Now Donna cannot speak—she is completely alert, but she's trapped in a body that will not respond. She can communicate only by moving her eyes. Thirty-three years old. What do you say when you bend over to speak to somebody in that condition? The medical community is uncertain. They don't offer hope.

But there is a God in Heaven who does not lie. He said, "I am the resurrection and the life. He who believes in me will live, even though he dies" (John 11:25). Paul wrote that "In all things God works for the good of those who love him, who have been called according to his purpose" (Romans 8:28). That's our only real hope. Because one day we're all going to be in that condition. Maybe not at 33. Maybe at 93, or maybe at 23! Our rope is going to break; our body is going to give way. What will we hold on to then? It's important we have the truth of Jesus Christ. Only His promise will be sufficient.

Paul addresses his letter "to Titus, my true son in our common faith" (v. 4). The truth deepens affections. Most relationships in the world are superficial because the world puts "me first." Only in Jesus Christ do we begin to learn to put others ahead of ourselves. Our relationships deepen because we're not just acquaintances. We become brothers and sisters and mothers and fathers and sons and daughters in the same family of God.

For the last 14 years, Dave Kennedy and I have preached the same sermon almost every Sunday. When he lived in Louisville, we started doing a series of sermons together. When he moved to Danville, Illinois, we agreed we would continue to share illustrations, outlines, Scripture verses, and ideas on the telephone. The best by-product is our relationship. I see Dave only three or four times a year, but he is an intimate friend. He knows enough about me to ruin me, but he wouldn't dare because I could destroy him in a minute! (He's a University of Illinois basketball fan and a UK fan. Believe me, you can't get a worse combination than that.) Yet he is probably my best friend. Our common commitment to the truth of the gospel of Jesus Christ binds us together; he's my true brother in the faith.

The truth enhances our personality. It gives us "grace and peace from God the Father and Christ Jesus our Savior" (v. 4). Generally speaking, the older people get, the crankier and the more worrisome they get—unless they are committed to Jesus Christ. Then the older they get, the more graceful and peaceful they become—because they know there's still hope.

A missionary to the Kiamichi mountain Indians in Oklahoma told of driving up to a shanty where an elderly Indian squaw sat in a rocking chair on the front porch. He called out to her, "Are you all alone, Ma'am?"

She just grinned a crinkly grin and said, "Just me and Jesus, son, just me and Jesus."

Though people may get older and alone, they don't have to be lonely. They can be full of grace and full of peace as they get closer to the truth.

It's important that we have a knowledge of the truth. It gives us a sense of purpose. It improves our character. It solidifies our hopes. It deepens relationships. It enhances personalities. It is just what our world needs.

## The Responsibility of Truth

We have a responsibility with the truth, and that's simply to share it as it is. "He brought his word to light through the preaching entrusted to me by the command of God our Savior" (v. 3). The truth has been entrusted to us and we have been commanded by God to share it. But it's important we understand that the truth is God's message, not ours. If I send a letter by the U.S. Mail, it's the mail service's task to deliver that letter intact. They're not to change it, alter it, or add to it. I don't care how they get it there, by air or by truck or by foot, but they're supposed to get it there as I wrote it.

God has entrusted His message to us. We can use different methods, different music, different buildings, and different kinds of programs, but the message of the truth is not to be altered. It is not ours. Mother Teresa said, "I'm just a little pencil in the hand of God, who is writing a love letter to the world."

"What I received I passed on to you as of first importance" (1 Corinthians 15:3). "If we or an angel from heaven should preach a gospel other than the one we preached to you, let him be eternally condemned!" (Galatians 1:8). "See that what you have heard from the beginning remains in you. If it does, you also will remain in the Son and in the Father" (1 John 2:24).

In spite of those admonitions, churches are inclined to dilute the message or to add to it in one way or the other. Seminaries that once stood firm for the basics of the gospel now begin to question the validity of the Bible and challenge the authenticity of the miracles. Conventions of major denominations approve of homosexual ministers, when the Bible says that's an abomination to God. Or they change the wordings of familiar prayers or hymns so that it won't sound chauvinistic; "Our Father who is in Heaven" becomes "Our Father and Our Mother" or "Our Creator." Publishing houses that once printed the truth begin to adjust their message so as not to alienate people who are more liberal in their thinking. The teaching that Jesus is the only way to God is pushed aside so that more material can be sold. Local churches that once stood firm on the basics of the gospel begin to thin their language about sin so they won't offend people; they present Jesus as a good friend who can make them wealthy and happy.

A recent editorial in *Christian Standard* told that during the Revolutionary War a group of soldiers camped out on a field near a farm house. It was cold. The soldiers needed wood for a fire. The officer in charge saw a wood rail fence. He knew the men needed to keep warm, but he also wanted to respect the property of the owner. So he told his men they could take off the top rung of the fence, but only the top rung, for firewood. When the officer awoke the next morning, to his dismay he discovered that the fence was completely gone. It was all the way down to the ground, and yet not one soldier had disobeyed his order. They had all taken just the top rung. When scriptural principles begin to erode, it's not long before there's nothing of substance left to restrain the evil of the world.

Why do churches dilute the message? Why don't we stand firm? One reason is human pride. The world has a cunning way of making people who stand for absolutes to look ignorant and uneducated. "You mean you want creationism taught in the school? How backward." "You mean you're against abortion? Boy, you're in the minority." "You mean in your church women don't serve as elders? Oh, are you behind times!" "You really think people should go through the ritual of a marriage ceremony before they have physical relationships? Come on, these are the 90's." "You mean you're teaching in seminary what the kids learn in fifth-grade Sunday-school class? That's not very fresh." We don't want to appear out of touch, so we adjust our theology to keep our pride.

The second reason we dilute the message is that we think it will enhance its appeal. We're afraid that if the truth is too demanding it will scare people away. Maybe we're asking too much of people to believe in miracles like walking on the water. Maybe it's too demanding to ask people to negate their sensual desires. Maybe we're asking too much of people to stay with their marriage even if they're not happy. So we accommodate the message to broaden the appeal. But the sad irony is that a diluted message actually loses its appeal because people are hungry for the real thing. People know down deep something is drastically wrong with this world and we need repentance. When the gospel is shared in its purity and its original challenge, it has awesome power. "The Word of God is living and active. Sharper than any double-edged sword, it penetrates even to dividing soul and spirit, joints and marrow; it judges the thoughts and attitudes of the heart" (Hebrews 4:12).

I got a telephone call from a reporter from *Time* magazine. "I've heard about your church," she said, "and I want to ask you some questions about why your church is growing rapidly while many mainline denominations are losing members."

I tried to point out to her that it was God that made the church grow and some reasons why I thought this church was growing. "There may be a number of reasons why mainline denominations are losing members," I said, "but I think that one primary reason is that there has been an erosion of belief in the integrity of the Bible. People are hungry for absolutes. If they come to church knowing that the Bible has those absolutes and they don't receive them, they go away hungry. And as starving people, they're going to begin to look someplace else to be fed."

> "The days are coming," declares the Sovereign Lord,
>    "when I will send a famine through the land—
> not a famine of food or a thirst for water,
>    but a famine of hearing the words of the Lord.
> Men will stagger from sea to sea
>    and wander from north to east,
> searching for the word of the Lord,
>    but they will not find it" (Amos 8:11, 12).

That is why it is important that as a church we stand firm in the truth; that those of us who teach and preach tell the truth, God's truth, the whole truth, nothing but the truth. That means you have a responsibility to the truth, too.

Be discerning. Don't buy it just because it comes from this pulpit or from a Sunday-school teacher. Always align the truth spoken to the plumb line of the Word of God.

Be supportive. If the truth is being proclaimed, then use your resources to see that it can be shared abroad.

Be studious. Paul told Titus that a knowledge of the truth leads to godliness. Don't be satisfied to sit in the pew and swallow once a week when you're spoon fed. Learn to study on your own so you can grow ten times faster.

Be courageous when opportunities arise for you at work or school or in your community to speak up for the truth. Stand firm in the truth; don't cower, don't apologize for it. Just speak the truth in love.

Be confident. There is tremendous power and appeal in the simple truth of God's Word. You don't have to cram it down people's throats. You don't have to get upset if they don't believe it. Just lay it out there. In its simplicity it has convicting power.

Most of all, be consistent. Live the truth. William Barclay said, "A man's message will always be heard in context with his character." If the truth is going to have any power through you, there's got to be an authenticity and transparency about you that makes the truth appealing.

My wife asked me to stop over to a woman's home to pick up some cookies she needed. So I stopped and met the woman.

She said, "Are you Bob Russell?"

I said, "Yes, I am."

"You know, I listen to you preach on the radio every Sunday. And I just want you to know that I really appreciate your messages," she said. "The thing I appreciate about your messages is that you are not afraid to stand for the truth the way you see it. Not everybody does that."

I got so caught up in her perceptiveness that I left without paying for those cookies. I didn't think about it. When I got home, I looked at the box. It said $12.50. I couldn't call her back fast enough. I said, "Mrs. Griffin, I forgot to pay for those cookies."

She said, "That's all right. I've heard you preach enough that I knew you'd call back."

I started thinking, "Boy, what if I hadn't seen that and hadn't called back?" If I hadn't called back, my message would have meant nothing at all. That's why 1 Timothy 4:16 says, "Watch your life and your doctrine closely. Persevere in them, because if you do, you will save both yourself and your hearers." If you claim to be standing for the truth, you'd better try to back up that claim with a consistent life or it's nullified. "Stand firm. Let nothing move you. Always give yourselves fully to the work of the Lord, because you know that your labor in the Lord is not in vain" (1 Corinthians 15:58).

Remember the words of Martin Luther's hymn, "A Mighty Fortress Is Our God":

And tho' this world, with devils filled,
Should threaten to undo us;
We will not fear, for God hath willed
His truth to triumph through us. . . .

Let goods and kindred go,
This mortal life also;
The body they may kill:
God's truth abideth still,
His kingdom is forever.

Paul said, "I'm writing to God's elect by faith." You're the elect of God when you leave the falsehood of this world and put your faith in the truth of Jesus Christ. He said, "I am the way and the truth and the life. No one comes to the Father except through me" (John 14:6).

# Choose Your Leaders Carefully

## Titus 1:5-9

MARK KILROY GREW up in a good home and was a medical student at the University of Texas. He had a keen mind and a bright future. One night some friends invited Mark to go out for a good time, and he went bar-hopping with them. That night, he fell under the influence of leaders of a Satanic cult, who later turned on him, attacked him, tortured him, mutilated his body, and killed him. Mark's remains were found several days later on a farm near Brownsville, Texas, along with a dozen others.

That incident ought to remind every young person, and all of us, of the importance of choosing our leaders carefully. Mark Kilroy is not alive today because he made a wrong choice about the people he would follow. Most of the time, the consequences are not that immediate or dramatic. But the result of choosing wrong leaders can be eternally disastrous.

Paul wrote to Titus about the importance of appointing right leaders in the church. He counseled Titus about how to direct the affairs of new congregations that had been established on the island of Crete. He wrote, "The reason I left you in Crete was that you might straighten out what was left unfinished and appoint elders in every town, as I directed you" (Titus 1:5). The churches were growing; they had great potential, but they needed proper leadership.

It is crucial that the church select qualified overseers. Anyone who knows anything about the dynamics of leadership knows that two or three people can make a significant difference in the direction of a large body. An appointment to the Supreme Court is carefully scrutinized because everybody knows it is an appointment for life, and it's a position that can determine the nation's future. The nine individuals sitting on that bench can be like the rudder of a large ship that determines its direction.

This passage before us has both a specific application, and a general application. The specific application is to us as a church; we need to choose our leaders carefully. The general principle is to all of us individually: we need to choose our role models carefully. Only Jesus Christ is worth worshiping, but we all need role models. We all need people that we look up to. It may be an athlete, it may be a school-teacher, it may be an entertainer, it may be somebody we work with, but we all have people who influence us. We need to be careful about the people we follow.

## The Function of Church Leaders

Paul urged Timothy to be selective in the kind of men he appointed to leadership in the church. The church leader is designated here as an elder. Now elder did not necessarily mean "older" chronologically, but older in spiritual maturity. An elder "must not be a recent convert, or he may become conceited" (1 Timothy 3:6). People grow spiritually at different rates. It normally takes several years and a number of experiences before a man would be considered spiritually mature enough to be an elder. Paul had established these churches on the island of Crete just two or three years prior to the writing of this letter, so they couldn't have been too old spiritually. But according to verse 7, the function of an elder was to be an overseer, responsible for the direction and the spiritual management of the church.

A perceptive observer says that in the Bible the elders had

five responsibilities. One was to preach (1 Timothy 5:17); another was to teach (1 Timothy 3:2); another was to shepherd the flock, to guide and protect the flock (Acts 20:28); another function was to pray effectively, particularly for the sick (James 5:14); and finally, they were to determine the doctrinal stance of the church (Acts 15). But in the modern church, we ask the elder to do five things. One, go to church Sunday morning. Two, go to church Sunday night. Three, go to church Wednesday night. Four, give an offering. Five, go to board meetings. And we'll settle for three out of five.

But an elder is to be an overseer by teaching, preaching, shepherding, managing, and praying. He doesn't have to perform every one of those functions, but he does need to show gifts in those areas before he is appointed. Someone should not be ordained an elder simply because he has paid his dues and we want to reward him with a spiritual leadership role. Just because someone comes to church regularly and he tithes and he's a nice person, does not mean that he should be a shepherd. Ephesians 4:11 says that God gives different gifts to people; one of the gifts He gives is the gift of pastoring, the gift of shepherding or leading. The church needs to ordain spiritually mature people who have leadership gifts.

Henry Ford said, "The question of who ought to be the boss is like asking who ought to sing tenor in the quartet." Obviously, the man who can sing tenor ought to sing tenor. You can appoint me a tenor in the quartet, but that doesn't make me a tenor. You can appoint a person as a shepherd in the church, and that doesn't make him a leader if he's not gifted to be a shepherd. So, the elder's function is to be the shepherd, the guiding person in the flock.

Three things about the function of the elder are contrary to popular thought. These are not popular ideas, but I think they're scriptural. First, *the elder is a male role and not a female role.* Paul says that the elder ought to be the husband of one wife, the overseer of his family. Some suggest that Paul was just accommodating the culture of his day, but since the Scripture designates the elder as being a man, we have only men serve as elders in our church. Other positions of leadership and involvement in the church are open to females, but the role of elder and the role of deacon in our church are male roles. It is not a matter of superiority, it is a matter of us being submissive to the authority of God's Word in this issue.

I heard about a man who came across an accident. A woman was bending over and attending to the needs of one of the victims. The man rushed over, shoved the woman aside and said, "Here, let me at him. I've had a course in first aid."

The woman stepped back and said, "Well, when you get to that point in your course where it says, 'call a doctor,' I'll be right here."

Some men just think they are supposed to take over; they're superior. That's not the case at all. I don't know why God designates in His Word that men are to be the elders in the church, but I can think of two reasons. One is scriptural and the other is just my speculation. The first reason the woman was to be submissive in this world is because she was the first to sin. That was a reminder of her sin (1 Timothy 2:14). The second reason is that I think the male ego is so weak that we have to be in charge; if we're not in charge, we bail out. But whatever the reason, as we try to let the Scripture be our guide as best we can, we have men serve as elders.

The second thing that goes against popular thought in this passage is that *the church is a Christocracy, not a democracy.* Growing up in America, we think we're going to determine everything by popular vote. But Paul didn't tell Titus to hold a congregational meeting. He said, "Titus, I want you to appoint elders in each town." Now we're not told specifically in Scripture what nominating process is to be used in the church. God gives us flexibility there. But we're not always supposed to have a popular vote.

In our church, the elders serve as a nominating committee, and they try to select men who are spiritually mature and gifted to lead. These men are then set before the congregation for the congregation's approval. Under that system, it is rare that a man would not be approved, but the congregational response does give a good reading of the leader's respect. It underscores, also, that the church is not a democracy in which we try to sink to the level of the average spirituality of the people. It is a theocracy, a Christocracy, in which we try to select the more spiritual leaders to lift us up to the mind of Christ.

The third thing about the function of the eldership that goes against modern thought is that *there is a plurality of pastors and not a single pastor.* Paul did not say, "Timothy, I want you to select one man in every church. He will be the pastor and everybody is supposed to follow him." He said, "Titus, you appoint elders, several spiritual men to lead the congregation." The Lord did not establish a pastor-ruled church. He instructed that there be several, a plurality, who were elders or pastors. The preaching pastor is one of those elders, but not the only one. "The elders [plural] who direct the affairs of the church well are worthy of double honor, especially those whose work is preaching and teaching, for the Scripture says, . . . the worker deserves his wages" (1 Timothy 5:17). The elder who preaches and teaches is worthy of being paid a living wage, but he is just one of a number of elders who are to oversee the church.

I do not run Southeast Christian Church. This is a hard concept for some on the outside to understand, but Southeast Christian Church is not "my" church. My task is to be the pastor who preaches and teaches God's Word. The responsibility for the oversight of this church rests on 23 other men who are overseers, or elders, from the congregation.

Someone left me a message that said, "Would you tell Brother Bob that there are dandelions in the front church yard?" Those are not my dandelions. About 5,000 people own those dandelions. It's my task to preach and teach God's Word. It's the elders' task to oversee the church. It's the elders' task to take care of the dandelions. It's my job to accept their gift and go to Hawaii! We split the responsibilities!

I have a good spirit of cooperation with the elders. They acknowledge my gifts and they are very supportive. I acknowledge their delegated authority and I try to be submissive. They know my weaknesses and they try to compensate in those areas. They are not rubber stamps; they ask tough questions. They make the staff and me account for every dime that we spend, and they register some objections. We need that for the church to be strong. God in His wisdom has provided that the church be directed by a plurality of spiritually mature men.

## Qualifications of Church Leaders

Paul underscores the qualifications for leadership in the church. He says, "An elder must be blameless" (v. 6). I don't know of anybody who is completely blameless, but I think "blameless" means, "not subject to damaging accusation that's going to embarrass the church." *The Living Bible* paraphrases this verse, "must be well thought of for their good lives."

Paul also points out that their *family relationships* should reflect spiritual maturity. An elder is to be the husband of but one wife. Now some take that to mean that he's never to have been divorced and remarried. Most conservative scholars interpret it to mean "a one-woman man." He should have a solid commitment to his wife, and he's not to be a womanizer. He is to be sexually pure.

In your role models, look beyond the charisma and worldly success. How are they doing at home? If they don't exhibit a moral integrity there, maybe you should back off. Paul says an elder is to be a man whose children believe and are not open to the charge of being wild and disobedient. You can tell a lot about a man by observing his family. If his children are out of control, rebellious, or if they never come to church; if he goes to the PTA meeting under an assumed name, then don't follow him as a leader. If Christianity doesn't work in his home, he isn't ready to lead in the church.

At the same time, be realistic. Everybody's children rebel on occasion. Every child goes through a transitional phase. Billy Graham's children are believing, but he had a son who was rebellious for a period. Franklin turned his back on Christianity, but in recent years he has returned and has a significant ministry. I think Billy Graham would have made a serious mistake if he had backed off from preaching while his son was going temporarily through a period of rebellion. There has to be an evaluation of a person's effectiveness over a period of time. When a child grows up and leaves home, the parent no longer has control and should not be held accountable for the choices that that child makes independently. But the overall family life of the elder should reflect God's will for the home.

An elder's *social life* is also important. He should relate well to other people. He must not be overbearing. The King James Version says he is not to be "self-willed." Some people are so domineering that they try to lead by intimidation.

Bill Weedman has preached in our children's church for several years. He's not an ordained minister; he's a policeman. The children love him so much, they have often requested that he baptize them. Bill carries a gun with him almost everywhere, as policeman do.

Once when Bill was going to baptize a child, he went into the changing room and saw another man who was going to baptized that same day. Bill took off his jacket and the man just stared at his gun.

Without changing expression, Bill said, "We have a 'no back out' policy about baptism." That guy couldn't get into the baptistery fast enough!

That's a little overbearing. We're not to lead by intimidation.

Have you ever gone on a trip with somebody who is domineering? It's got to be their restaurant, their route, their schedule. You let them lead because you're afraid of offending them or incurring their wrath. Don't follow a person who manipulates you like that. Inevitably they'll make you miserable or take you where you shouldn't go.

An elder must not be quick-tempered. If a man has a volatile temper, he'll make rash, angry decisions and be divisive in meetings.

He should not be given to drunkenness and violence. Think about all the violent things done in our society as a result of drunkenness.

A few years ago, a drunk driver plowed into a school bus outside of Carrollton, Kentucky, killing 27. Ever since that time, there's been an outcry against Ford Motor Company for making unsafe buses. Not much outcry against Anheuser-Busch for making an unsafe beverage.

A winery worker in California slit the throat of his wife and six other people, including his own children, and put them in a garbage dump. His friends said he had been drinking beer, wine, and tequila.

An oil tanker spilled millions of gallons of oil along the Alaskan coastline killing wildlife, destroying the environment and the economy. The ship's captain was drunk when the ship went off course and ran aground. There were all kinds of protests against Exxon Oil for negligence. Not much protest against Gallo Wines or the Miller Brewery.

Ninety-five people were crushed to death at a soccer match in England. According to the London Times, drunken hooligans trying to get in without a ticket caused the chaos.

Drunk drivers kill 25,000 people a year.

A nominee for the President's cabinet was rejected by his peers in the Senate because of a reputation for excessive use of alcohol.

On and on it goes.

When are the American people going to be honest enough to say, "We've got a serious problem—not just with drugs, we've got a bad problem with alcohol"? We need to quit promoting it on television and we need to quit serving it at college football and basketball games, and serving it at our wedding receptions and parties. I'm not sure the American people have the fortitude to make such a choice, because most of us are so involved in drinking, we don't want to make the sacrifice.

But church leaders ought to be distinctive. We have an opportunity to say by example, "that's enough." The Bible says a church leader is not to be given to much wine, not to be drunk. In our church, we go a step further and we ask our elders to be total abstainers.

Because of our example and because of the devastating consequences in our society, it really is wise for a growing Christian to reach the point where you say, "I don't need that. I'm going to walk the high road." Don't say, "I'm sorry, I don't drink." Don't apologize for it. Just say, "No thank you, I'll take a coke." Senator Mark Hatfield says when he sits down in a restaurant, he immediately turns the wine glass upside down just as a signal that he doesn't drink.

I wish I could quote a Scripture verse that said, "You shall not drink." But even though I don't have the authority of God's Word to command you, I encourage you to become a total abstainer. I have never known a person to become a teetotaler and later regret it. The Bible says, "Do not get drunk with wine, which leads to debauchery, but be filled with the Spirit" (Ephesians 5:18). I believe that the more you are filled with God's Spirit, the less you need alcohol. The church leader especially is not to be drunk or to be violent.

An elder is not to pursue dishonest gain. If a man cheats other people in the business world, he's not to lead in the church. He has lost his reputation.

An elder must be hospitable. *The Living Bible* paraphrases that, "they must enjoy having guests in their homes." An elder must be approachable. Open up your home sometime. Once a month, have somebody in from the church that you don't know as well as you do those three or four people you're always associating with. Just have pie and coffee, or pizza and ice cream—something that really goes together —and just get to know each other a little bit. You'll discover that in an hour's time in your home, you get to know people better than you do in six months of looking at the back of their heads in church.

An elder's family life is important. His social life's important. So is his *personal life,* his character. He is to love what is good. He shouldn't just love people. He should love the truth and try to maintain a balance between standing for truth and being tolerant of people. It's easy to love people if you don't care about truth, and it's easy to be dogmatic in standing for truth if you don't care about people. But it's tough to maintain that balance between standing for the truth, and at the same time being compassionate to people.

An elder needs to be holy and self-controlled. People don't expect their leaders to be perfect, but they do expect them to be authentic, to be honest, and to try; not a model of perfection, but a model of growth.

## Convictions of Church Leaders

"He must hold firmly to the trustworthy message as it has been taught" (v. 9). A church will remain doctrinally sound if the church leaders remain doctrinally sound. One of the blessings and refreshing things about Southeast Christian Church is that we have people coming from every background imaginable spiritually. That's refreshing because we have to dig in and really examine what the Bible has to say. It's essential that the leaders of the church maintain a common doctrinal stance.

It is important that we choose our leaders carefully, and that we monitor their lifestyle and their beliefs carefully. Unlike Jesus Christ, who is the same yesterday, today, and forever, people change. Jim Jones, I'm sure, had a lot of good beliefs when he first started. But his influence apparently went to his head and he got off course. People followed him blindly without monitoring where he was. It's a mature Christian who can say, "I admire that person, but there are certain areas of his life that I don't agree with." Or, "I used to really follow that woman but now that she's changed so much, she doesn't influence me any more." Paul tells leaders to hold firmly to the truth that was taught to them. Don't waver on that.

"Encourage others by sound doctrine." We usually think that doctrine is boring and discouraging, but in a world where everything is falling apart and caving in, it is encouraging to be able to say, "Here's where we stand. Here's what the Bible says. It may not be popular, but this is where we're going to stand." That's encouraging. That's refreshing, because it's a foundation of truth.

Look at the last phrase: "Encourage others by sound doctrine and refute those who oppose it" (v. 9). Refuting wrong doctrine is something that doesn't seem to matter when everything's going smoothly, but when difficulties arise in the church it becomes really important, and the time to prepare for that is now.

Once in a while, it is necessary for Christian leaders to take a stand against eroding truth. A shepherd doesn't just feed and love. A shepherd sometimes has to protect against wolves. We all prefer to be positive, but at times it is essential for a leader to confront error. It needs to be done as lovingly as possible, but repeatedly in Scripture the elder is told to rebuke and to refute if necessary. "Preach the word; be prepared in season and out of season; correct, rebuke, and encourage—with great patience and careful instruction. For the time will come when men will not put up with sound doctrine" (2 Timothy 4:2, 3).

Most Christian people find confrontation distasteful. We hate disagreement so much that if we're not careful, we'll compromise on our principles just to maintain harmony. I've seen leaders take a stand against evil and immediately, other Christian people react against them as though they're the ones at fault because they are rocking the boat. If church leaders have to confront evil, don't immediately oppose them. Look at the issue. Maybe there is a principle that needs protecting. Respect the leaders enough to listen to their position without bias. It is their responsibility to stand for the truth, even if sometimes it means unpleasant confrontation or dismissal.

A preacher came to me really discouraged. His youth minister had impregnated a young girl in the congregation.

Several months later they got married, and the youth minister asked to remain as youth director in that church. The preacher and several of the elders thought that the youth minister should resign because he hadn't set a good example for the young people. Even though they forgave him, they felt it would take a while for his credibility to be reestablished. Several of the elders and the father of the girl thought that they ought to just forgive him. Everybody makes mistakes. Let him continue to serve as youth leader.

No decision was reached. The young man continued on as youth leader. Several people left. The elders were divided. The preacher and the youth minister barely spoke, and the church stagnated. In my opinion the elders should have taken a firm stand and said to the young man, "Although we forgive you, there's a certain credibility necessary for a leadership position. We're going to ask that you step down. As you establish credibility over the years, perhaps you'll have similar position in the future." But because no decision was made, and because of a fear of upsetting the people in the church, it became a festering boil in that congregation.

There come times when leaders have to confront issues and make tough choices. It may mean refuting someone who gains sympathy because he looks like the underdog. But nothing undermines the stability of an organization like the feeling that nobody is in charge here.

Once the leaders make a decision and a recommendation, it's the duty of the congregation to be submissive to it. "Obey your leaders and submit to their authority. They keep watch over you as men who must give an account. Obey them so that their work will be a joy, not a burden, for that would be of no advantage to you" (Hebrews 13:17).

For example, when Paul was preaching on the island of Cyprus in Paphos, they converted the mayor. But the mayor had a sidekick named Elymas, a sorcerer, who opposed Paul. "Paul, filled with the Holy Spirit, looked straight at Elymas and said, "You are a child of the devil, and an enemy of everything that is right! You are full of all kinds of deceit and trickery. Will you never stop perverting the right ways of the Lord? Now, the hand of the Lord is against you. You are going to be blind" (Acts 13:9). And instantly for a period of time, he was blind.

If you had been there when Paul refuted that man, would you have come to the man's defense? "Paul, that's not very loving. This poor individual." If you had, you would have been wrong, because Paul was filled with the Holy Spirit at a time when he needed to rebuke that man so that the gospel would spread and the church could continue to grow.

It is important that we choose leaders wisely, as a church and as individuals, because when difficulty comes, when Satan mounts a frontal attack, it's essential that our leaders are men who understand their role. Men of character. Family men who stand strong for the truth. Only then can the church continue to be distinctive as the people of God seeking to grow to be like Jesus Christ.

It's been said that a good leader is able to inspire people to have confidence in him, but a great leader is able to inspire people to have confidence in themselves. A Christian leader is able to inspire people to have confidence in Jesus Christ completely. Only He is worthy of our worship. He said, "If anyone would come after me, he must deny himself and take up his cross and follow me" (Matthew 16:24).

# Guard Against Legalism

## Titus 1:10-16

PRIOR TO WORLD War II, France developed a line of defense along its eastern border called the Maginot Line. It was a massive buildup of guns, ammunition, and fortification of every kind. France was determined to thwart the inevitable invasion from Germany. But when Hitler's attack came, the Maginot Line was unsuccessful in stopping the German blitzkrieg. Actually, most of the enemy did not come across the French-German border at all. In March of 1940, Hitler's forces came around the Maginot Line and invaded through the Netherlands, Belgium and Luxembourg. France fell within two months because of an inadequate war strategy.

Today, most Bible-believing churches are digging in against liberalism, and rightfully so. Basic moral values are under attack. The integrity of the Bible is being questioned. We need to stand firm in the faith because the faith that was "once for all entrusted to the saints" (Jude 3) is the only faith that promises eternal life. But while we dig our trenches to resist a frontal assault from liberalism, we need to be on guard against legalism as well. Satan is described in the Bible as a cunning adversary. He will go to any length to destroy the church. And while liberalism threatens the discipline and the sense of purpose in the church, the blitzkrieg of legalism destroys the morale and the spirit of the Lord's army. "The letter kills, but the Spirit gives life" (2 Corinthians 3:6). That's why Paul warned Titus to beware of false teachers, especially those of the circumcision philosophy. As a church, and as individual Christians, we need to avoid both extremes.

Let's look at the problem of legalism and then analyze its cause, its consequences and its cure.

## The Problem of Legalism

The dictionary defines legalism as "a strict or excessive conformity to a law or moral code for the purpose of self-exaltation." Spiritually, legalism occurs when people impose human tradition or opinion on themselves or others. Its basis is human achievement. It is an open denial of God's grace. We have trouble sometimes understanding that Christianity isn't only a religion. Christianity is a relationship with Jesus Christ. A religion is an attempt to reach God by obeying a certain system of moral values. But Christianity is accepting God's forgiveness for our sins and relying on His grace. Christianity is the worship of the person of Jesus Christ.

But legalists still believe that God's favor is going to depend on our exact obedience to rules. That idea doesn't come from the New Testament, it comes from their tradition. Legalists love a list of do's and don'ts, and judge others by their obedience to their arbitrary code.

Jesus encountered both the liberals and the legalists. The Sadducees were the liberals of that day. They denied much of the Old Testament. They didn't believe in life after death or many of the miracles. But the Pharisees were the legalists. They demonstrate the problem of legalism in the New Testament. They were the most demanding, insensitive, selfish people Jesus encountered. Jesus hardly ever had a good word to say about the Pharisees. He called them "blind leaders of the blind," "vipers," and "hypocrites." They were a brotherhood of narrow-minded legalists who were determined to reduce religion to a list of do's and don'ts.

To the Pharisees, the Old Testament wasn't explicit enough. They had to elaborate and give details in the Talmud as to what the Old Testament really meant. For example, the Old Testament said that they were to remember the Sabbath day, keep it holy, and not do any work on the Sabbath. But that wasn't enough for the Pharisees. They gave details about what was work and what was not work. The Talmud said you couldn't walk more than 7/10 of a mile, or that would be working. If you got off your donkey at dusk, you couldn't take off the saddle if it was the Sabbath day, because that was work. If a hen laid an egg on the Sabbath, it was not right to eat that egg because the hen was working on the Sabbath. If a man had a sore throat on the Sabbath, he couldn't take any medicine because he was practicing being a physician.

One group of Pharisees actually had a debate over what they should do if they remembered that they had forgotten to say grace an hour after meal time. Should they just stop where they were and have a retroactive grace, or did they have to go back to the very spot where they ate and say grace there?

The Pharisees hated Jesus because He was free and he didn't adhere to their laws. They were always critical of Him. "Why aren't you fasting the way we do? You and your disciples have too much joy, Jesus," or, "Why are you healing people on the Sabbath? This is not a day for work," or, "Why are you eating with sinners and publicans? Does that mean you're not any better than they?"

Jesus said to them, "You tie up heavy loads and put them on men's shoulders" (Matthew 23).

Legalists are almost always critical of people. Some of the most vicious people in the family of God are the legalists whose rules you don't keep. It's not enough that their own lives are insensitive, arrogant, and joyless; they want these same standards for everybody else.

Paul encountered the problem of legalism, too. "There

are many rebellious people, mere talkers and deceivers, especially those of the circumcision group," he said (v. 10). They are called Judaizers elsewhere in the New Testament. These were people who insisted that a person must first become a Jew before he became a Christian. If a man was a Gentile, he first had to be circumcised before he could become a Christian. If he were already a Jew and he became a Christian, he had to keep observing the Sabbath, refrain from eating pork, and observe all the Jewish feasts, or he wasn't really a Christian. Paul rejected that idea as being completely erroneous. "Pay no attention to Jewish myths or to the commands of people who reject the truth" (v. 14). It is not Jesus plus something else, it is Jesus only that saves.

We still encounter the problem of legalism today. Some churches get so legalistic that they capture weak and new Christians and stifle their spirit. A church in Tennessee established a policy years ago that all the men in their church had to keep their hair short because the Bible says that nature tells you a man shouldn't wear long hair. So they described what was short: "Any man whose hair goes beyond his collar will not be welcomed within ten feet of the Communion table." When women started wearing pantsuits, churches established dress codes for women that said, "Women are not to come to church in slacks." It wasn't enough that the Bible said, "Dress modestly." They had to set a rule defining modesty. A church in Kentucky had a rule that its preacher could not use any other translation of the Bible other than the King James Version in the pulpit.

Can you remember dogmatic Christians getting upset a few years ago when men started wearing beards and mustaches? They would talk to these men about setting a bad example, showing a spirit of rebellion. Now we laugh about that, because some of you look pretty woolly and nobody says anything about it.

I can't laugh at those legalists too much, because when young men first started wearing earrings, I kind of gravitated back to a dogmatic stance: "I'm just going to insist that no young men in our church can wear earrings because that's a sign of rebellion and it's effeminate."

Somebody said to me, "The pirates wore earrings years ago and they weren't very effeminate."

I said, "Well, that's different!"

Styles change, but legalists aren't very flexible. We can't be dogmatic about somebody else's style. I tell my boys they can wear earrings if they're big enough to whip me and pay all their own bills. But I can't be arbitrary about what somebody else does.

It's incredible how legalism can infiltrate a church and cause us to establish rules. There are all kinds of rules. Every service must end with an invitation. No tapes or records can be sold in the vestibule of the church. No taped background music or drums on Sunday morning. No speaker from a denomination other than our own can speak from the pulpit. No one who is divorced will be married in this church. No musical instrument will be used in worship. People must be baptized on Sunday morning publicly. The preacher must not drive a red car, it hurts his testimony.

I'm not suggesting that churches should have no policies at all, but churches should be careful that local policies are rare and they never become equal with Scripture in authority.

It's not just churches that have problems with legalism. Sometimes individual families have problems too. Legalists establish all kinds of extrabiblical rules in the home. Don't go to the movies. Don't practice mixed bathing. Don't go to the beach on Sunday. Don't dance. Don't play cards. Don't belong to country clubs. Don't buy raffle tickets. Now maybe we shouldn't do some of those things, but each individual, each family, has to decide for itself. These rules become a problem when we don't distinguish between opinion and Scripture, and our opinions become the standard by which we gauge the spirituality of others.

I went to Bible college with a young man who was so legalistic, he thought it was wrong to drink a cup of coffee because it had caffeine in it. He came from a very conservative background. He was one of those guys who would not call a card table a card table. It was a folding table or a game table. He didn't want anyone to think he played cards or gambled. But somebody pointed out to him that the cola he liked to drink had caffeine just like a cup of coffee did. That devastated him. He nearly drove himself crazy for fear that he was going to do something wrong.

Two things happened to him that mellowed him. Number one, he got married. He learned that human beings are imperfect and that he was imperfect. Second, he began to preach and to love people, and slowly, that concern for people mellowed his spirit. A friend saw him recently and said he was even laughing at himself a little bit.

There's not much joy in the life of a legalist, and there's not much authenticity either, because if you believe that you are going to earn God's favor by keeping rules, you're always frustrated. If you think your spirituality is determined by how well you keep the rules, there's a constant temptation for you to cover up who you really are.

## The Cause of Legalism

Paul gives two reasons why people are motivated to be so rigid. One is *selfishness*. They do it for the sake of dishonest gain. I think some media preachers take a dogmatic stand because they know a certain segment of rednecks out there will support them financially because they're "telling it like it is." Sometimes a dogmatic position makes people feel secure and superior. They have a grasp on truth that nobody else does.

A second motivation is *a poorly trained conscience.* Paul says, "Their minds and their consciences are corrupted" (v. 15). Your conscience can be programmed wrongly in your youth. I know of a woman who had it drilled into her so much when she was a young child that she was not to call anybody "a fool." She thought it was wrong to say that somebody was foolish; that was one of the worst things you could say, she thought. That's foolish! Her conscience was programmed wrongly. Your conscience can be programmed with all kinds of legalistic ideas about what's the right kind of worship, what is proper entertainment, when you should laugh, and how you should spend your money. Even if intellectually you know what is right, you keep gravitating back to what your spiritual mentor or what your parents told you. You keep hearing voices in your conscience.

I can add two other causes for legalism. One is a natural *overreaction to liberalism.*

One of our men was telling me he was really concerned that his boys not be effeminate. He wanted masculine sons. One day his boy was carrying around a purse. It really disturbed the father, and he bolted out of his chair and grabbed that purse and threw it in the garbage and swatted the kid on the bottom and said, "Now, you're not going to be effeminate! I don't want you carrying around a purse!"

The boy was crushed. Then the mother came in and said, "Jim, that's his doctor bag he was carrying around."

We see moral values eroding because of liberalism and we erroneously conclude that the best way to counter liberalism is extreme fundamentalism. I know of a church on the east coast that has a sign in the vestibule that reads, "No woman shall speak beyond this point." It's a very small church! The leaders were overreacting against a trend in many churches where the women serve as elders. I can understand why John MacArthur described fundamentalism saying, "It's not much fun, it's not much mental, sometimes." But Satan would have us overreact and have us establish man-made rules that will stifle the church.

One other reason that people are legalistic is *a dogmatic interpretation of certain passages of Scripture.* For example, on the last night of His life, Jesus instituted the Lord's supper. He said, "Do this in remembrance of me" (Luke 22:19). But also on the last night of His life, Jesus washed the disciples' feet. He said, "I . . . have washed your feet, you also should wash one another's feet" (John 13:14). Why do we observe the Lord's supper regularly, but we never wash anybody's feet? It's because we go through the rest of the Bible and we find the early Christians regularly observing the Lord's supper, but they did not observe foot washing as an ordinance. They understood that Jesus meant it to be an act of humility, an example of servanthood toward each other, not an ordinance to be practiced in the church. But if you look only at that passage in the Book of John, then you have foot washing as an ordinance in the church.

We believe the Bible to be the Word of God, rightfully so. We are to properly divide the word of truth, according to 2 Timothy 2:15. The Bible is its own best interpreter. The Bible, as the Word of God, doesn't contradict itself. If you have an interpretation of a passage of Scripture that contradicts another passage of Scripture, you've got the wrong interpretation.

Another rule of interpretation in the Bible is, "literal if possible, figurative if obvious." Most of the Bible is not too difficult to understand, but some of the Bible is figurative language and some of it is cultural in context. Sometimes it is difficult to tell the difference. For example, a passage in 1 Corinthians says that women shouldn't cut their hair because it's a disgrace. It was a disgrace because in Paul's culture, women who cut their hair were women of the street. Styles have changed; it is no longer a disgrace for women to cut their hair, The principle doesn't change; their appearance is to be modest. But a legalist can take that one passage of Scripture and say that women should never cut their hair. Legalists fail to make any distinction between figurative and literal language and they become extremely dogmatic.

We must be careful, though, that we don't dismiss a block of Scripture casually by saying it's just cultural or figurative. The rule is "literal if possible, figurative if obvious." Let's say your boss left for a week and he gave you a list of ten things that he wanted you to do, and at the bottom of the list he said, "I want you to work your fingers to the bone." You know that's figurative—he doesn't expect to come back and see skin worn off your fingers. But just because one statement is figurative you don't dismiss the other ten things and say, "I'm not going to do any of it," or else you'll be looking for a new job.

We also need to be careful we don't label everyone who doesn't agree with us in one camp or another. Have you ever noticed how we label people? Somebody who drives faster than you is always a maniac. Everybody who drives slower than you is an idiot. Only your speed is right! We do the same thing in the church. If someone disagrees we say, "He's a legalist; she's liberal; he's a Pharisee; they're dogmatic." We need to maintain some flexibility in those areas of interpretation. A good rule is, "In doctrine unity, in matters of opinion liberty, but in all things love."

## The Characteristics of Legalism

Since they posed a danger to the early church, Paul described the legalists to Titus in unflattering terms. They are "rebellious," Paul said (v. 10). They were rebelling against the very concept of grace, which is the heart of the gospel.

"They are mere talkers," said Paul. Often legalistic people talk a good game because they're very outspoken against sin, but they don't back up their talk with their lifestyle. One television evangelist was always hounding away about immorality and adultery and pornography. Then the media disclosed that this evangelist was himself meeting prostitutes in a motel. Watch out for the crusader, for the Christian who's always riding the hobby horse. Often the very sin they're obsessed with is the one they're indulging in.

Paul said, "To the pure, all things are pure, but to those who are corrupted and do not believe, nothing is pure" (v. 15). In other words, if some people see evil in everything, it tells you where their hearts and minds really are. Paul says that they are deceivers. On the surface they appear spiritual, and their rules seem to promise to lead to a life of purity, but actually just the opposite occurs. Rules don't restrain disobedience, they stimulate it. Have you ever gone by a bench that says, "Wet Paint, Don't Touch"? What do you want to do? Do you wonder if it's really wet? You'd never think of touching it if it didn't say, "Don't do it."

"When we were controlled by the sinful nature, the sinful passions aroused by the law were at work" in us (Romans 7:5). The law sometimes even aroused sinful passion. Sometimes people don't even think about what's wrong until they're told, "Don't do it." One Sunday I told my congregation about a woman in a church nearby who takes her keys out of her pocket and starts rattling the keys when, in her opinion, the time's up and the preacher should quit preaching. You know what happened then? It wasn't three minutes before some people were rattling their keys. They would never have thought about doing that if I hadn't mentioned it.

I heard about a preacher on the west coast who announced that he had listed every possible sin—there were 354 sins. He got letters from all over the country asking for the list. I guess people didn't want to miss out on anything. In Colossians Paul writes, "Since you died with Christ to the basic principles of this world, why, as though you still belonged to it, do you submit to its rules: 'Do not handle! Do not taste! Do not touch!'? These are all destined to perish with use, because they are based on human commands and teachings. Such regulations indeed have an appearance of wisdom, with their self-imposed worship, their false humility and their harsh treatment of the body, but they lack any value in restraining sensual indulgence" (Colossians 2:20-23).

I went to camp years ago with a legalistic dean who started out the week with a whole list of rules for the teenagers. One of them was, "No girl could wear shorts more than six inches above the knee." That's all they talked about all week long. The girls talked about how long their shorts were. Boys were volunteering to measure them. It was a bad week. I went to another week of camp where the dean had more wisdom. He said to the teenagers, "We want everybody to dress modestly. If you wear something that I think is improper, I'll tell you." And he did on a couple of occasions, privately. But the young people didn't think about it as much and they gave more of their attention to the essentials.

Legalism is deceptive. It looks good. "We're going to play

straight. We've got all these rules." But it lacks value in restraining evil.

Paul points out that legalism is divisive. He said, "They are ruining whole households by teaching things they ought not to teach" (v. 11). Some of you have real tension in your homes. Your parents are upset because you're worshiping in a church that's not the same denomination that you grew up in. Or you have Christian friends, or brothers and sisters, who wonder about your salvation because you're singing and using an instrument or because you're in a church that doesn't observe the Lenten season. I know of a church that dropped $12,000 a year support of a new congregation because the minister of that church called himself a pastor in the church paper. The supporting church thought he ought to be termed "the evangelist," so they dropped their support. Imagine the kind of anger and division that created. Legalists are always trying to impose their values on others. They can create a real stir because of their outspoken approach and their deceptive spirituality.

## The Cure for Legalism

Paul was emphatic that legalism must be confronted quickly. "They must be silenced," he said (v. 11). Don't be naive about legalism and assume that it will go away or that it's just a minor threat or that we need it. Be perceptive enough to recognize that it threatens the spirit of your family and your church. When legalism surfaces, confront it. "Rebuke them sharply," Paul says. He did. He didn't mince any words. He said, "Even one of their own prophets has said, 'Cretans are always liars, evil brutes, lazy gluttons.' This testimony is true. Therefore, rebuke them sharply" (vv. 12, 13), so they will be sound in the faith—not to put them down, but to restore them.

I got a phone call from a man I'd never met before. He said, "I know that your church supports this missionary work in New York City, and I want to tell you what's going on there. Do you know they have an elder in the church there who is not married? You know that the Bible says an elder is supposed to be the husband of one wife." The implication was that he wanted me to use my influence with the mission committee to drop support.

Now if that had happened years ago, I would have said, "Well, I'll look into that. I understand your concern." But I immediately said, "Before you go any farther, let me tell you something. I'm that missionary's biggest fan. Second, if you're saying that a man can't serve as an elder because he's not married, you're disqualifying Jesus Christ and the apostle Paul from leadership. And in the third place (I always speak in threes), that church has only about 50 people. They have to make some concessions in order to survive."

The conversation ended abruptly. But I think my rebuke may have forced that man to at least consider his legalistic position and to mellow.

Now if you're not a leader and you don't know much about the Bible, or if you don't know the legalists well enough to confront them, Paul said don't pay any attention to it; just disregard it. "Pay no attention to Jewish myths or to the commands of those who reject the truth" (v. 14).

Legalism is most effectively dealt with when we emphasize our freedom in Christ. Romans 12:21 says, "Do not be overcome by evil, but overcome evil with good." Let others see a joy and a freedom in your life. "Where the Spirit of the Lord is, there is freedom" (2 Corinthians 3:17).

Don't flaunt your freedom to deliberately antagonize people. If you've got a next door neighbor who believes it's wrong for you to work on Sunday, don't get up at 7:00 a.m. and wash your car underneath his window and sing "Amazing Grace" while your washing the car. The Bible says, don't let your freedom be an occasion to offend others. But don't apologize for it either.

If you find legalism creeping into your own life, do two things. Number one, work on a proper balance of attitude. On one hand, stand firm in the truth of the Bible, and on the other, be flexible in matters of opinion. Work at the kind of balance in your life described in this prayer: "Lord, help me to be steadfast but not stubborn, tactful but not timid, serious but not solemn, loyal but not sectarian, gentle but not hypersensitive, tenderhearted but not touchy, conscientious but not a perfectionist, disciplined but not demanding, holy but not self-righteous, discerning but not critical, progressive but not pretentious."

The second thing you need to do is be sure you have a proper concept of God. How do you envision God? As a tyrant, ready to strike you every time you disobey? Or as a loving Father, anxious to forgive and restore you? Your concept of God will make a big difference in whether you live in fear or you live in freedom.

Louis Hines wrote an essay about the first time he found out what his father was really like. As a little boy he admired and respected his father, but he feared him a little bit too. He was sitting in church right beside his dad. It was a hot and drowsy day and he couldn't stay awake. He started to nod. Out of the corner of his eye, Louis said he saw his dad's arm rise and he thought his dad was going to strike him or shake him. But his dad reached out to put his arm around Louis and draw him to himself. Louis Hines said he looked up at his dad and smiled. His dad winked back at him, and Louis just nestled in his dad's arms and went to sleep.

If you view God as an angry tyrant ready to strike you every time you fall short, your life is going to be full of fear. But Jesus said, when you pray, pray, "Our Father in heaven, hallowed be your name" (Matthew 6:9). Jesus said, "Do not let your hearts be troubled. . . . In my Father's house are many rooms" (John 14:1, 2). Jesus said that God is like a father who runs to welcome home a wayward son and who smothers his repentant speech against his shoulder. The Bible says, "Perfect love drives out fear" (1 John 4:18).

Allow God to put His loving arm around you and forgive you and comfort you. For the Bible says, "Where the spirit of the Lord is, there is freedom." He offers you freedom from guilt and sin and death and the law.

# Model the Truth

## Titus 2:1-3

THE ISLAND OF Crete had to be a dreadful place to try to build a church. People who lived there were "liars, evil brutes, lazy gluttons." At least that was one of their own prophets' descriptions of his homeland. The people of Crete were pagan, and spiritually hardened, but Paul and Titus had established a church there and it was growing.

After Paul had left the island, he wrote instructions to Titus to set the church in order. In the first chapter of Titus he instructed his associate to stand firm in the truth, choose leaders carefully, and be on guard against legalism. In Chapter 2, Paul emphasizes the importance of setting a positive example for younger Christians who have just been introduced to Christianity.

It's not enough that we just proclaim the truth; we are to model the truth in our lives. People learn much better by example than they do by instruction.

One of General Patton's soldiers told about a time when they were marching across Europe and came to a swollen river. The soldiers began to complain there was no way they could cross the raging current carrying their backpacks. Patton said nothing, but he waded into the river himself and swam to the other side with his backpack on. Then he swam back, waded back into the river, turned and looked back at his men and said, "Follow me." Without protest, every one of the men in the battalion followed him across to the other side.

One of the greatest needs in the church today is for positive role models. We're inspired more by example than we are by instruction, but many of the popular heroes of our day are seriously deficient. The athletes are into gambling or drugs. Politicians and entertainers are into egotism or dishonest gain. Religious leaders have been disclosed as hypocritical or self-centered. If the church is going to be strong in our pagan culture, it needs some mature Christians who inspire people by their walk with God.

In Titus 2, Paul gives instructions to three separate groups of leaders in the church.

## To Teachers

He tells anybody who teaches, particularly Titus himself, "You must teach what is in accord with sound doctrine" (v. 1). He's speaking to anybody who's a Sunday-school teacher or a youth sponsor, to those of you who teach in the educational system, and to anyone who is trying to instruct others in how to live. James wrote, "Not many of you should presume to be teachers, my brothers, because you know that we who teach will be judged more strictly" (James 3:1). That may not be a good verse to use when we're trying to recruit many new teachers and children's workers, but that's what it says: Not many of you should be teachers, because you're going to be judged more strictly.

When you first accept a teaching position, there's some glamour involved. It's exciting to think that you're going to affect people's lives. People compliment you and encourage you. But it's not long before the glitter wears off. You find out it's hard work to study every lesson, and people don't compliment you much after a while. If you're an adult teacher, they may even criticize you. If you're a children's worker, they may take you for granted.

Then one day it hits you: "This is a serious responsibility.

This is a long-term commitment. And if I don't make a change, I'm going to be doing this for the rest of my life." One day, it also hits you: "Some people are actually listening to what I say. And this message is making a difference in some of them!"

Early in my ministry people would come to me and say, "Thank you so much for that lesson. It really changed my attitude! I'm going to be a different person from this day on!" I wanted to say, "Well, I was just preaching, don't take it all that seriously." But then I began to understand—the Word of God is powerful. It can change lives. Anybody who teaches it or preaches it has a serious responsibility. God is going to hold us accountable for what we say. We're going to be judged more strictly.

Why would anybody want to teach if teaching has that kind of responsibility with it? It's because God has called us to teach. The Bible says God has equipped some people to become pastors and some to become teachers. I think more people are called to teach than do. God would not bless the church with an abundance of children without equipping many to lead them. Paul wrote, "I am compelled to preach. Woe to me if I do not preach the gospel!" (1 Corinthians 9:16).

We teach because we care about people. Maybe it's not the most glamorous position, but it is the most rewarding. If the gospel really saves people, if Christ really changes people for the better, then we can't help but share what we know. Even if it's risky. "Christ's love compels us, because we are convinced that one died for all" (2 Corinthians 5:14). We teach the gospel because we want to be found faithful in the duty that the Lord has given to us.

A teacher has a dual responsibility. The first is to *teach accurately*. "Teach what is in accord with sound doctrine." If you begin to alter the teachings of the Bible when you teach, you are usurping the authority of God and endangering the eternal destiny of your students.

During the air traffic controllers' strike, there was a shortage of controllers. One pilot radioed the tower and asked for permission to land, and the controller said, "Delta 288, you are cleared to land on Runway 9." But just moments later he heard the same controller say, "United 248, you are cleared to land on Runway 27."

The pilot immediately radioed the tower and said, "Tower, you just cleared me to land on Runway 9, and you cleared United to land on 27. That's the same runway, opposite directions, east and west. We're coming right at each other!"

There was a long pause. Then the controller said, "Y'all be real careful out there now, you hear?"

We're dealing with life-and-death matters. We're dealing with Heaven and Hell. We can't just be casual with our teaching as if it doesn't matter. The Bible instructs us to be diligent and faithful in our study of the Word. "Even if we or an angel from heaven should preach a gospel other than the one we preached to you, let them be eternally condemned!" (Galatians 1:8) We have to teach it accurately.

Second, we have to *live it faithfully.* "In everything set them an example by doing what is good. In your teaching show integrity, seriousness and soundness of speech that cannot be condemned, so that those who oppose you may be ashamed because they have nothing bad to say about us" (vv. 7, 8). If you teach the truth, some people are going to oppose you. They do not want to hear that they are accountable to God. They do not want to hear that there are absolute standards of right and wrong. They don't want to hear that they need to be faithful in their marriage. Paul tells us to expect that and to silence them by your life. Live in accordance with what you teach, so that they will be ashamed because that they cannot find something bad to say about you.

A newspaper article about Glenn Davis, the all-star baseball player for Houston, says that Davis had made a small but significant stand against the advertising of beer in radio and TV commercials for his team, the Houston Astros. One spring, Davis approached the team's general manager and expressed his distaste over what he perceived as his implied endorsement of alcohol. He learned from friends that every time an Astros player hit a home run, the radio and television broadcasters who covered the team would offer a toast from one of the commercial sponsors: "Glenn Davis, this Bud's for you."

Davis doesn't drink, and he said he didn't like being linked to beer consumption at the ball park. "I know they put a lot of money into this industry," he said, "but as a player, I feel I have a right not to associate with it. I spend a lot of time teaching young people not to drink, and I don't want to be seen as a hypocrite in their eyes."

Davis said his beliefs were influenced in part by his own experience. As a 17-year-old boy in Jacksonville, Florida, he and two other youths were almost killed in an automobile accident where they were all drunk. Davis made his case public because he thinks professional ballplayers are role models for youths whether they like it or not. "It comes with the territory," he said. "I think it's the duty and responsibility of every citizen in this country to be concerned about it." Larry Dierker, the broadcaster, said he has honored Davis' wishes even though he did not agree. But avoiding beer plugs when Davis hits a home run will no doubt affect Budweiser, the beer sponsor. Davis had hit eight of the Astros' fourteen home runs at that point in the season.

Whether you like it or not, you are a role model for somebody. If you're going to teach and claim to be a Christian. then you have a responsibility to be consistent with what you say.

## To Older Men

"Teach the older men to be temperate" (v. 2). By "older men," Paul is not necessarily referring to somebody who has one foot in the grave. Paul is talking to mature Christians; those who are older in the faith. You may be 40 or 50 or you may be a senior citizen, but you influence younger Christians.

Teach the older men to be temperate, he says. The King James Version translates that to mean "sober." *The Living Bible* says "serious." It doesn't mean you can't laugh, but it means that you take life seriously. You realize that there is something more than the next ball game. There's something more than the next fishing trip or golf game. There's something more than the next horse race in your life. Young men of the church need to see Christian men who can laugh and have a good time, but who can also pray and talk about their faith.

Be worthy of respect. In Oriental cultures, older people are automatically respected. Grandparents are revered and are taken into their children's homes and looked to for counsel. But in our culture, we idolize youth and vitality. Paul Harvey talks about the old man who put braces on his false teeth so he would look younger! Ads for hair color say, "Put this on and it will return your hair to its natural color." Gray's not natural?

We worship youth and vitality. We don't put much value on wisdom and experience. We tend to show disrespect for aging people and laugh at them. If you're young, don't ridicule old people. Don't mock the way they walk or ridicule the way they drive. Remember one verse whenever you're tempted to do that. The Bible says, "You reap what you sow." Unless you die young, you're going to be there someday, and the tables will be turned on you.

In the church, regardless of the culture, we're to show respect for older people. If you're an older Christian, Paul says, be "worthy of respect." Make it easier for people to respect you by being self-controlled. The word is translated elsewhere as "sensible." Such people are not overwhelmed by sudden wild alarms. They remain level-headed. They can have a steadying influence on others. *The Living Bible* says, "Be unruffled." Be sound in the faith.

Be sound in the faith. Some young Christians are vulnerable to every new spiritual fad. "Shirley MacLaine believes in reincarnation. Do you think that's true?" they say, or "What about this new doctrine about the second coming?" They need to be able to say, "I'm not sure what I believe about that. I don't have enough knowledge. But I respect some of the older Christians in the church, and they don't waver." They're not tossed about by every wind of doctrine.

Practice love. There's a tendency for some older Christian people to get crotchety, super dogmatic. But a Christian should become more unselfish and more compassionate with age and have a positive influence.

Practice endurance. We've got a dangerous practice in America called "retirement." It's a blessing in some ways, but it's also dangerous because it implies that your productivity stops when you get to be 62 or 65. It's dangerous in the church because people look forward to retiring so they can get out of all responsibility and relax and travel. While you may want to refocus your interests and redirect your involvement in the church, don't quit. Don't drop out of all responsibility. Don't turn it all over to the younger generation. We need the vitality of youth, but we also need the example and the wisdom of those who are older.

If you came to Southeast Christian Church during the week, you'd be inspired by many retired people who perform invaluable service to this church. Every Monday morning, one of our older Sunday-school classes, the Friendship Class, comes in and cleans the sanctuary. Some pretty sophisticated people are picking up gum wrappers, straightening up the books. Retired people are working in the yard, maintaining the vehicles, serving on the Tally Committee, setting up chairs, cleaning the sanctuary, greeting at the door. They have taken the focus off self and put it onto service.

The Bible has many examples of people who kept enduring until the end. Abraham's wife Sarah was 90 when she gave birth to Isaac. Moses was 80 when he led the children of Israel out of Egypt. Caleb was 85 when he conquered the hill country in Palestine. Simeon was an old man in the temple when he held the baby Jesus in his arms.

History has all kind of examples that people don't lose their purpose when they turn 62. Picasso was past 75 when he dominated the art world. George Bernard Shaw was still writing plays when he was 90. Michelangelo did some of his best painting after 80. Norman Vincent Peale is 90 and still preaching. Bob Hope is past 80 and George Burns past 90, and they're still entertaining. Ronald Reagan was president in his late 70's.

If God permits you to live long, continue to serve and be an inspiration to those who are younger. Matthew 10:22 says, "He who stands firm till the end will be saved."

## To Older Women

"Teach the older women to be reverent in the way they live" (v. 3). *The Golden Girls,* a situation comedy on television, is based on the premise that it's funny when older women are irreverent. Just the opposite is true. Once you get over the shock factor, not much is humorous about raunchy old women. But there is much that is attractive about poised, classy, respectful, spiritual older women who are faithful to the Lord.

Paul says, teach the older women "not to be slanderers" (v. 3). Gossip is a temptation for everybody, but it's a particular temptation for older women. They sometimes have more time and opportunity for it once their children are gone. When we spread malicious tales that hurt reputations, it sets a terrible tone for younger Christians.

When somebody comes to you with a juicy bit of gossip, saying, "Let me share something with you, and don't tell anybody," you just say, "Sure, it will be just as safe with me as it was with you!" Be an example of talk that edifies and encourages people. "Do not let any unwholesome talk come out of your mouths, but only what is helpful for building others up according to their needs, that it may benefit those who listen" (Ephesians 4:29).

Older women should be taught not to be "addicted to much wine," Paul says (v. 3). Stuart Briscoe wrote, "The older women who turned to drink, as many of our soap operas document daily, are usually desperately lonely women who have no significant involvement in life. They feel unwanted and useless, grovel in feelings of inferiority and irrelevance, and show their inner disgust and loathing by carefully calculating self-destructive behavior."

I know of a Christian woman whose husband died after she had retired. She was despondent. Completely out of character, she started to drink. She would drink during the day to boost her spirits, and she began to drink before going to bed so that she could relax. Her friends saw a personality change in her, but they didn't know what was causing it. Eventually, she drank every day and lost her positive influence and her ability to serve in the church. She was not a good example to the younger women.

Maybe you are hiding a drinking problem. You think you are getting by with it because other people don't know. You tell yourself that you don't have a problem. You can quit any time. Besides, you still function; you still go to work, you still drive the car, you still go to church. You just need a little boost to get you through the day.

I've never been a drinker, but I can understand how it can happen. One winter I had the flu. I never take medicine, but I was feeling so bad I couldn't sleep at night. My wife got me some liquid cold medicine. I didn't know anything about it, so I took some. In a few minutes I just zonked out and didn't wake up till about 7:00 in the morning. I came in to church and said, "Boy, I took some stuff last night that was great!"

The staff said, "Sure, it's 25% alcohol."

I didn't know that.

Some of you got started innocently enough. Just a glass of wine with a meal, just a relaxer before you go to bed. The Chinese used to have a saying, "A man takes a drink and then the drink takes a drink, and then the drink takes the man." You may have discovered that now you're dependent. You have to have it every day. You may have your family or friends hinting that you need some help, and you resent that. You're not a drunk. You're not looking for a place to sleep in some shelter downtown.

I encourage you today to make a change. Say, "It's gone far enough. I'm going to contact AA, or my minister." Do it for your own sake, do it for the sake of your family, but most important, do it for the Lord and for your testimony to Him. Alcoholism is the one disease that has to be self-diagnosed to be treated. Scores of respected individuals have been smart enough to say, "I am developing a dependency that I cannot control, and I'd better get help now or it's going to conquer me."

God "comforts us in all our troubles, so that we can comfort those in any trouble with the comfort we ourselves have received from God" (2 Corinthians 1:4). If you've gone through trouble, you can be a help to other people. Nobody understands like someone who's gone through it. That's the principle behind support groups. If God helps you overcome a problem, you're in a unique position to help others who go through it. Younger Christian women are going to need your example and inspiration in the future. Don't let them down. Then you'll be in a position to teach what is good. We used to sing, "Let the beauty of Jesus be seen in me." Proverbs 31 says, "Charm is deceptive, and beauty is fleeting, but a woman who fears the Lord is to be praised. Give her the reward she has earned, and let her works bring her praise at the city gate" (Proverbs 31:30, 31).

More than 20 years ago I first read a book by Dr. J. Wallace Hamilton. One chapter in the book has always stayed with me. It was called, "How Long Is Your Shadow?" The "shadow" he was talking about is our influence on other people. It said that when we walk outside, we can't control our shadow anymore than we can stop having a shadow in the sun. We can't control our influence. When Simon Peter walked through the streets of Jerusalem, people tried to touch his shadow. We all exert an influence. We all have a shadow.

He made two points that have always stayed with me. First, your influence, for the most part, is unconscious. You're not conscious of your shadow when you walk down the street. You hardly even think of your influence on others, but it's there. We think we're going to influence people by performance or by intention, but in reality, we exert influence when our guard is down. We don't even think about it.

We say, "My kids are growing up, and I need to influence them. They're getting old fast." So we sit them down and talk to them about clean living, and about their belief in God, and how they ought to think, and we say, "There, I've done it. I've influenced my kids." Well, maybe we have, because everyone needs to have a heart-to-heart talk, but that's not really where the influence is. What really talks to our children is not the speech when we were trying to impress them, but our casual conversation when we're not even thinking about it.

Jesus said, "You are the salt of the earth." Salt is not noticed very much, but it makes a difference. Your influence is unconscious.

Second, your influence is almost immortal. Like the ripples that flow out from a pebble in the pond, your influence goes far beyond your ability to see. You touch one life, and then they touch another, and then another. Even a man's or woman's death does not destroy their shadow or stop their influence. J. Wallace Hamilton died in 1968, and I'm still influencing people by what he wrote. A person may write a book, or leave a will, or just leave a memory. But though his voice is silent, he goes on speaking in his lengthened shadow. Who knows how your life is going to influence somebody way down the road?

Back in the late 1800's, my great-grandmother got a divorce. In that day divorce was a terrible stigma, but she refused to quit in her testimony to the Lord. She got her three children dressed every Sunday and took them to church. One of those children was my grandfather, who became a leader in his church. My grandfather laid his hands on me when I was ordained and prayed for me. When my son is ordained, my dad will lay his hands on my son's head.

How much do my son and I owe to the shadow of a woman in the late 1800's, who very few people probably noticed?

Everybody is an omnibus in which all of his ancestors are riding. Remember that little rhyme, "I have a little shadow that goes in and out with me, and what can be the use of him is more than I can see." Indeed, more than we see.

What makes a shadow? The sun; light. What makes a positive, consistent shadow in our life? The Son of God, the light of the world. That's why it is important that we model the truth all the time. You have no idea who is touching your shadow.

Hamilton suggested that's why we're not going to be judged immediately when we die. We have to wait till Judgment Day when all the returns are in. Our life may be finished here, but its influence will go on after it's over. Not until the end can you know how your influence is registered in the total of the human race.

# Build Godly Homes

## Titus 2:3-5

LOU HOLTZ, NOTRE Dame's winning football coach, recently wrote a letter to the next generation. His remarks appeared in Time magazine as one of a series of ads from Volkswagen in which prominent figures in America are given the opportunity to pass on their ideas to those who will inherit the earth 100 years from now.

I was impressed that Lou Holtz's entire focus was on the need for traditional families. He said that the strength of any society was not in its wealth but in its moral values, which are developed predominantly within the family. If America is going to be a strong nation 100 years from now, he added, we cannot relinquish the training of our children to gang leaders and drug dealers. The local church and the parents of today's youth must take a commitment to excellence.

I believe Lou Holtz is right on target. Our nation will be only as strong as its homes. That's also true of the church. No wonder Paul wrote Titus about the importance of building strong family units in the church. If Titus was going to be able to carve out a solid church on the island of Crete, there would have to be solid homes. If our church is going to continue to thrive in the midst of a society with rapidly declining moral values, then we have to give constant attention to the development of Christian families.

Paul mentions seven qualities that a godly mother should demonstrate in the home. The rest of us can assist her in developing those qualities.

## Her Attitude Should Be Loving

Paul says that older women should "train the younger women to love their husbands and their children" (v. 3). To my knowledge, this is the only time in all of the Bible where the wife is told to love the husband. In Ephesians 5, husbands are told to love their wives, and the word for love is *agape,* which means doing the loving thing whether you feel like it or not. But here in Titus 2, where the wife is told to love her husband, The word is used for "love" is *phileo.* That has to do with friendship, feeling, delighting in one another. In that day, when so many of the marriages were arranged by the parents, it certainly would be hard at times for the wife to enjoy the husband. But wives are told to *phileo* their husbands. Learn to be friends. Take delight in each other. We are commanded to love one another, even though every situation is not ideal.

Sometimes it's easy to love your family. When you are first married, and your husband is romantic, it's easy. When the children are cuddly newborns, it's easy to love. But there are times when it's not easy to take delight in your family. When your husband plays golf for the third Saturday in a row and leaves you to work in the yard, or when he is abusive or thoughtless, it's difficult to love. Or when your child complains about what you have cooked or sasses you for disciplining her, it is not easy to love. But those are the times as a Christian mother that you are to make the effort and to nurture that kind of feeling and attitude.

In his book *Happily Ever After,* Bill Cosby says, "The ultimate challenge for a woman in marriage is to accept it for the rerun that it is, but to keep herself from canceling the show." Sometimes it is difficult to love, but we are commanded to do so.

The rest of us could make it easier for the woman to love

in the home. Children, you can make yourself more lovable by just doing little, thoughtful things and expressing appreciation. Most mothers aren't very smart. They may have a high IQ, and they may be brilliant when it comes to dealing with people, but when it comes to being a mother, they will do things that are beyond common sense. They're willing to nurse you when you're sick, help you with your homework when you're ignorant, comfort you when you're depressed, feed you when you're hungry, and clean up your room when you're lazy. And with just a little "Thank you" once in a while, just an occasional hug, they're all fired up and ready to do it again. It's so simple, you're dumb if you don't try to be just a little bit more lovable and take advantage of her on occasion.

Husbands, most wives will be responsive to you if you'll just do the little things. Be lovable. Give a phone call when you're late, or a card when you're gone, or a smile when you walk by her, or a touch on the arm, and she'll get all emotional about that. If you want to see her go crazy, whisper little things in her ear like, "You look nice today," or "I enjoy being with you," or "I love you." Amazing things happen to her. She loses all sense of reason, and she finds it easy to be thoughtful, generous, and loving in return.

One wife told her husband, "I'd like something romantic and impractical for our anniversary." So he bought her a lovely gold bracelet.

"This is wonderful!" she said.

"Well," he said, "one little four-letter word made me buy this for you."

"Oh, do you mean L-O-V-E?"

"No, S-A-L-E."

That may be practical, but that's not exactly loving and appreciative! Be alert to your opportunities to be more loving in the home.

## Her Character Should Be Self-Controlled

The King James version of this is "discreet." In other words, there is to be some restraint of emotion, some degree of reservation. *The Living Bible* paraphrases it, "live quietly and be sensible." The Christian woman should not be a "space-head." She should not be volatile, subject to explosive fits of temper or uncontrolled bursts of excitement.

You may say, "Wait a minute. I'm a sanguine temperament. I'm not the quiet type. I'm not reserved at all. I'm loud, emotional, and funny, but at least I'm not a bore." But Paul's not discussing temperament here as much as he is character. Regardless of your natural temperament, remain under control. If you're an extrovert, don't take it to extremes. If you're a big talker, learn when to be quiet. If you're subject to bursts of emotion, don't let those emotions lead you where you shouldn't go or say what you shouldn't say. Your husband and children need the security of seeing you under control. Don't fly off the handle when you get upset. Don't jabber on endlessly when you have nothing to say. Don't panic when the pressure's on and go to pieces and blame your family and God. When you keep your poise, mother, and practice self-control in stressful situations, you create a calm atmosphere in the home.

The rest of us can make it easier for the woman of the house to be self-controlled by not adding unnecessary pressure. When you see your wife begin to lose it, be sensitive. When the two-year-old dumps his chocolate milk on the new carpet, that's no time to say, "Why don't you keep him in the kitchen?" That's time to grab the towel, get down on your knees and help out. When you bring guests home unannounced, and the house doesn't exactly look like it's out of *Better Homes and Gardens,* that's no time for you to say, "How come you can't keep this place cleaned up?" It's time for you to say, "Honey, I'm sorry I brought people home unannounced."

It's important that men help create an atmosphere where self-control is easier to practice, and that's especially true if the mother works outside the house. Elsa House wrote, "The statisticians classify us as having a full-time job. They're wrong, of course. We have two full-time jobs. And, of the two, the one for which we receive a paycheck is probably the easier one."

When the woman of the house has spent the day with a demanding boss, uncooperative co-workers, cantankerous customers, or rambunctious students, she's not likely to be patient when she gets home. That's no time for you to bark out, "How come we don't have decent meals around here anymore?" or, "When are you going to finish the bunny costume for the school play?" or, "Hey, the dog messed up over here again. Would you take care of it?" Be alert to the pressures she faces in the home and give assistance. Make it easier for her to practice self-control.

## Her Morals Should Be Virtuous

It is absolutely essential to the well-being of children that the moral standards of the mother be respected. Children can survive a bad father, but they seldom survive a bad mother.

Women, Satan would tempt you to be impure, but if you are unfaithful to your husband or if you're unfaithful to the Lord, you not only endanger your marriage, you endanger the well being of your children. They need to see you set consistently the moral tone of the home. That's tough to do if your mind is being saturated with soap operas, cheap tabloids, or paperback novels all the time. "Whatever is pure, . . . think about such things" (Philippians 4:8).

One mother was determined not to allow her children to absorb all the violence on television. She had an agreement with them. When they watched a television program, if somebody got murdered or somebody got hurt, they had to turn it off. The average length of their television programs was about five minutes! She said, "As the television program was going on, you'd hear the kids chanting in the background, 'Please don't hurt him, please don't hurt him.'"

My mother did something when I was a young boy that I now take pride in. We had a lot of company and we were all in the living room, watching a program on our new television set. Something suggestive came on, probably something that would be considered mild today, like a kiss that lasted more than a half-second. But everybody got a little tense watching that program. My mother got up, flipped the television off, and said, "Let's talk." It was amazing—everybody started jabbering at once, as if nobody was really interested in that program at all. I was embarrassed by that then, but I'm proud now to be able to look back and see her moral courage. I never questioned where her values were. I never questioned her purity of thought or life.

The rest of us in the home can make it easier for her. Men, don't ask your wife to compromise her values by going places or doing things that contradict her conscience. Children, compliment your mother once in a while for her integrity. You're bragging on other kids' mothers for their cooking, their humor, their appearance. Do you ever say to your mother, "Hey, thanks for standing for something. I want you to know I really respect your Christian life." That's not easy to do. I hear a lot of people compliment their mothers *after they've died*. The time to do it is while they're alive and while they can appreciate it.

## Her Priority Should Be the Family

Her priority is "to be busy at home," Paul says. This is an important phrase, since there are so many working mothers today. Michael Gerkin and Walter Cobb did a study of over 1200 midwestern couples, and they discovered that the higher the husband's occupational status, the more likely the wife was to work outside the home.

I believe that if it is possible, mothers of young children should not have a job outside the home. I don't mean to put another guilt trip on working mothers, you've got plenty of that already. But I would encourage those with small children to consider not working outside the home.

Ask yourself some questions. Is it essential for you to work, or do you have an excessive desire for material things? Would your children be better off with fewer things and more of you? Do you work outside the home because it's really what you want, or because your parents have driven you to pursue a career and you don't want to disappoint them? Do you work outside the home because it's fulfilling and it makes you a better all-around person, or are you overly concerned about status?

Nobody can answer those questions for you, but if you can't answer them to your own satisfaction, then I encourage you to consider quitting your job and spending all your time at home. If you can answer them to your own satisfaction, then quit laying a guilt trip on yourself, but continue to make the home your first priority.

This passage does not say it's always wrong for the mother to work outside the home. My mother went to work when I was in sixth grade. Nobody in the family seemed to have difficulty with that except me. I had two younger sisters and younger brother. I resented my mother's job a little bit because I wasn't the center of attention as much as I had been. I came to realize that it was necessary for my mother to work, and it was also an expanding experience for her. She continued to work until retirement. I don't see being "busy at home" as meaning you should not have another job or outside interest.

I've known mothers who didn't have a career who weren't busy at home, either. They were busy on the golf course or busy at the club or busy watching soap operas.

The Bible has a number of examples of godly women who had careers. Lydia was a seller of purple, Esther was a queen; Priscilla worked making tents. The Book of Proverbs tells about a virtuous woman who was involved in real estate and merchandise.

An article in *Business Week* called "Mommy Track" suggested that some corporations are offering alternatives to career women. Women don't have to choose between being Superwoman and June Cleaver. They can work part-time if they have young children. Companies will make their schedules flexible so that they don't lose outstanding talent.

Whether you choose to have a career outside the home or not, make your family a priority. Find some way to be busy at home, which means making the home a priority and being the guider of the home. Let your family know that you consider nothing more important than their well-being.

And don't apologize for it if you don't have a career. Tony Campolo said that his wife had a Master's degree, but when the children were young, she chose to stay at home with her three children and not have a job. Her difficulty came when she would go to social functions and some career woman would look down her nose and say, "What do you do?"

She learned to say, "I'm socializing two Homo sapiens in the dominant values of the Judeo-Christian tradition in order that they might be instruments in the transformation of the social order, so that they might realize the eschatological potentialities of Utopia." Then she'd look at them and say, "What do you do?"

They'd say, "Oh, I'm just a lawyer."

Be busy at home. Make the home and your children your priority. The rest of us can help them do that, too. Husbands, don't demand that your wife have a career if she doesn't want to have one. Don't put her down by bragging about somebody else's wife who has an impressive career and makes a lot of money. Be proud of her contribution at home and reinforce that importance. If your mother works outside the home, don't put unrealistic demands on her.

Somewhere in the back of our minds, we have an unreal image of a perfect mother who does everything exactly right. She gets up at 5:00 a.m. and cooks breakfast. Bacon, eggs, toast and grits, biscuits and gravy. She serves it at 6:00 with a smile. She kisses her husband good-bye. She hugs her children before they go to school. Then she does the dishes with a smile. She sits down with her little ones and teaches them to read before 10:00. At noon when they take a nap, she's busy dusting and cleaning up the house so that it's spotless. Then at about 3:00 in the afternoon, she welcomes her kids home from school and sits down with them for about an hour to talk about their day. Then she starts making supper and greets her husband at 5:30 looking like she's just stepped out of *Cosmopolitan* magazine. They sit down at 6:00 and have a beautiful, well-balanced meal, all the family together. They sit and laugh and talk until about 7:30. Then she helps the children with their homework and tucks them into bed at about 9:00, and sits down for about an hour and a half and talks with her husband around the fireplace. When they go to bed at 11:00, she's humming, "When you come to the end of a perfect day."

If that's your image of a wife and mother, she's never going to measure up. Get real. These are the Nineties. No such mother exists or ever has. In some of the old time homes, children ate in another room and slept in the attic. They were to be seen and not heard. If you have a mother who really is busy at home, and makes you a priority, then overlook some of her imperfections and be grateful—and express your gratitude on occasion.

## Her Personality Should Be Kind

That virtue is missing in a lot of homes, isn't it? Ever wonder why we treat strangers with kindness and tenderness, but snarl continually at the people we're going to weep over the most when they die?

"Get it yourself!"

"Who was your slave last year at this time?"

Mother, I think it begins with you. The Bible simply says, "Be kind to one another." If your attitude is surly, sarcastic, and critical, then your home is not going to be a very pleasant place. But if your attitude is gentle, encouraging, and kind, then the home has a much better chance of being a place of peace.

One Sunday, my wife forgot that she was supposed to direct the Women's Chorus in church. She seldom forgets anything. She has a hard time sometimes understanding how I can forget things. But it had been an extremely busy weekend and she completely forgot that her chorus was providing special music for all three morning worship services. So, at the first service, the women's chorus sang and she wasn't directing it. She was at home in bed. Later she was really embarrassed for missing it.

Our church staff has a little styrofoam trophy called the "Oops Award" that we give away every week to the staff member who makes the biggest booboo during the week. The following Monday, after staff meeting, I had five pizzas delivered, and about 14 of us from the church staff dropped in on my house unexpectedly for lunch. Before lunch, we presented my wife with the "Oops Award" for the week, the first time we'd ever given it to a non-staff member.

She received it graciously, with a smile, and it was on display in our kitchen for a week. But to receive that is special. That's graciousness. That's rare. That's kindness.

That will never happen again as long as I work here, I'll assure you!

Much of being kind in the home has to do with sense of humor. Can you laugh at yourself when you goof up? Can you laugh when there's pressure on? Learn to be kind and gracious in the home. Learn not to put the heat on too much when somebody else makes mistakes.

## Her Role Should Be Servanthood

Young women are "to be subject to their husbands" (v. 5). That's her humility. It's a basic biblical principle that the husband is to be the leader of the home. Now that doesn't mean he's a dictator like Ralph Cramden, the king of the castle. It does mean that there is an acknowledged order in the home. It means that God has delegated the husband to be the leader and a tender-hearted lover. The wife is to respect his leadership. That may sound old-fashioned, but the amazing thing is that it works, at a time when so many modern partnership marriages are falling apart. I think God has created us in such a way that man's ego needs the assurance that he is the leader. And I believe that God has created us in such a way that no matter how talented or brilliant the woman, she needs the security of knowing that she is under an umbrella of protection.

The same principle is set forth in Ephesians 5:22, 25:

"Wives, submit to your husbands as to the Lord. . . . Husbands, love your wives as Christ loved the church and gave himself up for it." It's reiterated in 1 Peter 3:1, 7: "Wives, in the same way be submissive to your husbands. . . . Husbands, in the same way be considerate as you live with your wives." Women, you have a choice to make. You can try to build your home as the world does, saying, "This is a partnership. I have full rights. Nobody tells me what to do." Or you can say, "We'll try to build this home the way God has designed. When we have disagreements, I want to feel free to express my disagreements, but if we can't come to an agreement, I'll acknowledge your leadership." That takes humility. That takes submission to God's authority.

That attitude eliminates the constant tug-of-war, so prevalent in marriages, to see who's really in charge of the relationship. Gene Getz suggested that most women who have difficulty submitting to the husband have difficulty submitting to other authorities as well—the job, the church, the state—because her underlying attitude is not humility, but defiance.

Husbands need to assist her in doing that. They often go to two extremes. One is to try to be a dictator, but you don't help people follow by barking out orders. A more common problem than the dictator today is the wimp. A lot of women would love their husbands to take the lead and give direction, but the husbands and fathers make that difficult because they are so passive. I see guys who are executives make decisions and have authority at work, but when they come home and they're tired, they become apathetic at home.

When Dr. Clyde Narramore of the Rosemeade School of Psychology was asked, "What is the number one problem in counseling?"

"The passivity of the male," he said. "Centuries ago, a man fought off Indians, hunted for wild game, built log cabins, conquered the West, and was necessary for the survival of his family. Not so today. Nuclear missiles protect us from invasion. Food is picked up at the local store. Our homes have become houses that are merely commuter centers and sleeping places, and women are more independent from men than at any time in American history. So in modern times, the need for a male leader is not what it once was.

"Or is it? In truth, the need for a loving male leader in the home may be greater today than before."

Harvard scholar, Dr. Zimmerman, showed that every advanced civilization went into decline as the men became more passive and the women more dominant.

Wesley Epstein conducted a study of five family combinations of male/female relationships within the home. The study indicated that only the father-led type of family produces predominantly emotionally healthy children. Again, the biblical view of the family is accurate. But you know what that means—fathers and husbands have to be busy at home too. The family has to be a priority no matter how important you think your job is.

I know of an executive who, every night when he arrives home, just sits in the driveway for several minutes shifting gears. "Not the gears of the car," he says, "but the gears of my mind. I've been so preoccupied with business, I just sit there for a minute or two reminding myself that the people I'm going to meet inside are the most important people that I'm going to meet that entire day, so that I can give attention to my wife and children that they deserve."

## Her Motivation Should Be to Glorify God

Finally, her motivation should be that no one will malign the Word of God. There's no greater testimony to our faith in Jesus Christ than a Christian home. Skeptics can try to ridicule the Bible; they can make fun of television evangelists; but they will not ridicule a godly home. Over and over again, even unbelievers will say, "I wish my home were like that."

A mother's motivation is not just to convince the skeptics, however, but her own children, not to malign the Word of

God. Our primary purpose is to raise children who know Jesus Christ. If children sense that their mother is hypocritical, they'll grow up to malign the Word of God and ridicule the church. But if they know their mother's faith is genuine, even though she's imperfect, they'll grow up to respect the Bible and love the church.

Children, you can really help your mother do that. When she encourages you to come to church, don't make her drag you out of bed every Sunday morning. Cooperate. When she takes stands that tell you what you can and can't do, don't beg her to change her mind and tell her how old-fashioned she is, cooperate with her. And when you're faced with decisions, don't disappoint her by violating the principles she has taught you.

My son, keep your father's commands
   and do not forsake your mother's teaching.
Bind them upon your heart forever;
   fasten them around your neck.
When you walk, they will guide you;
   when you sleep, they will watch over you;
   when you awake, they will speak to you.
For these commands are a lamp,
   this teaching is a light,
and the corrections of discipline are the way to life.
                    (Proverbs 6:20-23)

# Plan for the Future

## Titus 2:6-8

I OFTEN WONDER what Southeast Christian Church will be like 30 years from now.

If I came back to visit in 30 years, how many people would be worshiping here? Would I be excited to see 10,000 people packing out four worship services, or would I be disappointed to find a handful of people rattling around in a large auditorium?

If I stopped to read the brochures in the vestibule, would I discover that the church had greatly expanded its ministry to the hurting in 30 years? Would there be a dozen more support groups really helping people who are struggling with various problems? Or would I find that the church had lost its compassion for people and was focusing on finances?

If I talked to the worshipers coming into church, would I find them excited about the church's outreach? Would they say, "We've started a new congregation of a thousand people and they're doing great. Our missionaries overseas are making a significant impact, and we've sent 30 young people out into full-time Christian service." Or would they be indifferent about evangelism outreach?

Would the people report to me, "You can't believe how much I've learned about the Bible; it's really helping me.

Wait until I show you what's going on in the Children's Department and the activities building. It's incredible the way this church is helping families stay together!" Or would there be a cavalier spirit about the Bible and an indifferent attitude toward the needs of youth?

It would be thrilling to come back in 30 years and see that people had been saved for eternity, families had been solidified, young people had been loved, older people had been ministered to, single people had received attention, and week in and week out, Christ had been exalted.

If those kinds of dreams are to be realized, then we must plan for the future. Somebody said, "If you aim at nothing, you'll be sure to hit it." Jesus said that no man building a tower will not first sit down and calculate the cost, and no king going forth to war would go into battle without first estimating his odds of winning. The church needs to have definite plans for the future. "To man belong the plans of the heart, but from the Lord comes the reply of the tongue" (Proverbs 16:1). In other words, we can make our plans, but the future is really in God's hands. He is the one who responds. But God blesses effort. Our plans may not be His plans, but His will comes to those who use their insight and diligently seek Him.

Look at Titus 2:6-8 with the future in mind. Paul was writing to Titus about how to build a church on the island of Crete. Here are three things we can do to make our church what it ought to be in the future.

## Develop Younger Believers

Paul said that the older women should "train the younger women to love their families," (v. 4) and in the same way, the older men need to "encourage the younger men" (v. 6).

One thing we can be certain of—the strength of the church in 30 years will rest in the hands of those who are under 45 today. I doubt if many of the current leaders will be serving as officers 30 years from now. If the church continues a dynamic ministry in the future, it is imperative that we train young people with a proper dedication to the church. The larger the church becomes, the greater that responsibility. "The things you have heard me say in the presence of many witnesses entrust to reliable men who will also be qualified to teach others" (2 Timothy 2:2). Pass on the baton to future generations, because the church is only one generation from extinction.

In one year our church added a college minister, a junior high minister, and an assistant in the Children's Department. That may seem like an inordinate amount of attention on young people, until you remember that 75% of the people who become Christian do so before they are 14 years old, and 95% of the people who become Christian do so before they are 21 years old. The wise church plans for the future by placing a great emphasis on developing the youth of today.

We are to train the young men to be self-controlled. Certainly young men are to be taught other things, but Paul mentions only self-control. Maybe Paul emphasizes this because the people on the island of Crete were out of control. Maybe he felt once they got a handle on self-control, the rest would be easy for them. The word *self-controlled* means sensible, level-headed; dictated to by God's Word, not by one's own feelings.

All kinds of outside influences would control our young people today. Some are controlled by chemicals. They're so driven by their desire for drugs and alcohol that they do senseless things. Some are driven by their craving for sex. They lose their sense of judgment. Some are driven by greed or desire for pleasure. They lose all common sense. Every one of us has one sin that will destroy us if we don't get it under control.

But we are to train our young people to be distinctive. They must learn that their primary mission in life is not to have fun, but to be obedient. They must learn that the primary mission in life is not to feel good, but to be good. They must learn that the will of God and His church comes before their own personal ambition. I've read that maturity is the ability to postpone pleasure. We need to train our young people to be like Moses, able to sacrifice the pleasures of this world for a season and be willing to suffer affliction with the people of God.

There are two essentials to training young people. The first is encouragement. Paul says, "Encourage the young men." Stuart Briscoe says that word *encourage* means, "persuade with authority." Don't just have a casual attitude when they're wrong, but use your authority and persuade them. Sometimes young people need chastisement. They need somebody to say, "That's wrong. We're not going to put up with that around here." But most of the time they need what educators call "positive reinforcement." Teachers have a slogan, "Catch 'em being good." If you encourage them when their behavior is correct, they'll be more likely to repeat it. That means you swallow your critical words sometimes and look for opportunities to boost them up when they do well.

One Sunday night recently, we ordained four young men into Christian ministry. Every one of those young men, in his remarks to the church, thanked the church for their encouragement. Some had written notes, some in Women's Circle sent cookies while they were in Bible college, some gave money, many patted them on the back. That encouragement motivated them.

We need that kind of encouragement all the time, not just for seminary students, but for all of the young people in the church, who are future leaders. What a responsibility they're going to have in 30 years! Encourage them when they have the courage to be baptized. Encourage them when they're in a musical. Encourage them when they do something well. Sometimes you're critical of the way young people behave in church. If some young people around you are behaving correctly, after church why not say, "Hey, I was really proud of you today, you did great!"

Young people also need to learn by *example.* "In everything set them an example by doing what is good" (v. 7). "Like people, like priests" (Hosea 4:9). In other words, a class is going to take on the personality of the teacher. A team is going to take on the personality of the coach. A church is going to take on the personality of the leaders of the church, the older people. That means we constantly have to be on guard, alert that people are watching our example and learning from it.

Somebody asked superstar baseball player Joe DiMaggio why he hustled all the time and never loafed. He said, "I'm aware every time I go out on the field that there is somebody in the stands who is watching me play for the first time. I don't want to disappoint them."

Christians ought to be motivated to give of their best every day, because there's always somebody observing you when you least expect it, and they're subconsciously imitating you. Often you don't know when other people are observing you. It seems I can't go anywhere without people seeing me. They say, "Hey Bob, I saw you on the expressway behind that older lady who wouldn't merge. You really got exasperated with her, didn't you?" "I saw you out at the basketball game at halftime when the girls' dance team was performing. You had your binoculars on them. I was watching you." Since people are watching, our best response is to give our best all the time, so we can encourage young people to be self-controlled.

## Anticipate Increased Opposition

Paul says we should live rightly, "so that those who oppose you may be ashamed because they have nothing bad to say about us" (v. 8). That doesn't mean the critics are going to be silenced and have nothing at all to say because you are so good. He is saying that you shouldn't give critics legitimate reasons for opposing you; don't give them ammunition. They'll have to manufacture shallow accusations or false charges like they did against Jesus, and that's embarrassing for them.

A Christian who legitimately lives a Christian life, or a church that's doing its job, is going to be opposed. Listen to what Jesus said: "If the world hates you, keep in mind that it hated me first. If you belonged to the world, it would love you as its own. As it is, you do not belong to the world, but I have chosen you out of the world. That is why the world hates you. Remember the words I spoke to you: 'No servant is greater than his master.' If they persecuted me, they will persecute you also" (John 15:18-20). The apostles were persecuted all the time. Paul was beaten, Steven was stoned to death, James was beheaded. Some of them were imprisoned. Some early Christians were thrown to the wild beasts in the arena. We aren't persecuted like that today, but if we do our job as Christians, some people are not going to like us. In fact, Jesus said, "Woe to you when all men speak well of you" (Luke 6:26).

Some opposition will come from people in the world. The world doesn't understand the kind of impact the gospel can have on changing people's lives. They're threatened by a dynamic church. They see lives changed and they don't want to change themselves. A Louisville man, several months ago, counseled with a local psychologist. The man was suffering from depression. He said part of his depression was due to the fact that some of his friends had become members of Southeast Christian Church. Their values had changed and he no longer identified with them.

The counselor said, "I think Southeast Christian Church is a cult, and Bob Russell is kind of like Jim Jones."

Now I've been preaching the same message for 20 years. Actually, it's 2,000 years old. But because the church grows large, and people don't understand it, they think it's a cult. A business that succeeds is not necessarily connected with organized crime, and a church that grows is not necessarily a cult. But I shouldn't be surprised at that. Jesus said, "Beware when all men speak well of you."

Some opposition will come from religious people. Jesus' most vocal critics were the Pharisees and the religious leaders because He didn't fit the mold. Some religious leaders resent a growing church. They label it a country-club church or they delight in finding something wrong.

A pastor of a growing church was accused by some fellow ministers of being a "sheep stealer" because believers were coming from other congregations. His classic reply was, "I'm not stealing sheep, I'm just planting grass!" When Christians aren't being fed, they look for a place where they can be nourished. It's easier for the congregations they leave to be critical than to change.

Some opposition will come from the media. Recent surveys have demonstrated that nearly 90% of national television reporters and newspaper editors come from a liberal persuasion. Only 10% attend church regularly as opposed to the national average of over 40%. So the media is not going to be very sympathetic to a Bible-based message. They have an awesome power to ridicule.

When respected author and psychologist Dr. James Dobson was the only person granted an interview by convicted killer Ted Bundy, the national media resented it. Some presented Dr. Dobson as a television evangelist who was in it for greed. The reason Ted Bundy granted Dr. Dobson the interview was because Bundy wanted to show the direct correlation between hard core pornography and his violent crime, and he wasn't sure that the normal media would print that. Dobson reported it. *Penthouse* magazine and *Playboy* magazine responded with articles in their publications trying to undermine Dobson's credibility and make him appear ridiculous.

Some opposition may come from the government. Our government is making an effort to completely separate church and state. In an effort to be value-free they are becoming anti-Christian. Jesus said, "If you're not for me, you're against me."

James Kirkpatrick, nationally known syndicated columnist, wrote an editorial recently about a woman named Evelyn Smith in Chico, California who refused to rent her duplex to a couple living together without being married. They sued her and the court ruled against Mrs. Smith and in favor of the unwed couple. She had to pay a fine to the plaintiffs, and also post a notice in her rental units confessing her violation of the law and promising not to repeat the offense, because California has a fair housing law. Kirkpatrick asked, "Why is it lawful for an unwed couple to lease her duplex, but unlawful for the same couple to share a room at the state university two miles away?"

Our government, bending over backward not to discriminate, is beginning to discriminate against people with convictions. In the next 30 years conservative churches may face some opposition from the government. Perhaps a church that would not admit members who are living together without marriage, or would not permit a homosexual to teach, or would not permit women to serve in every capacity, could lose its tax exempt status or be fined.

Persecution can come in a lot of different ways. We need to anticipate some opposition, and when it comes, we need to do three things. First, we need to rejoice. Jesus said, "Blessed are you when people insult you, persecute you and falsely say all kinds of evil against you because of me. Rejoice and be glad, because great is your reward in heaven, for in the same way they persecuted the prophets who were before you" (Matthew 5:11, 12).

When I learned that someone called me a Jim Jones, I said, "Give me his phone number. I'd like to talk to that guy!" But I'm not supposed to do that. I'm supposed to say, "Praise God, it's wonderful to be persecuted and opposed!" That doesn't seem normal, but Jesus said, "Be abnormal." When any kind of opposition comes, even a little thing, rejoice over it. The prophets and early Christians were persecuted for their beliefs. It's nothing in comparison for us to have to endure a little criticism.

The second thing we need to do is remember we're in good company. That's the way they persecuted Jesus; that's the way they persecuted the apostles; that's the way they persecuted the prophets, so we ought to rejoice. Paul Harvey says, "You always find the most clubs under the trees with the best apples."

Third, and most important, when we're opposed we need to keep our composure. Satan loves to get Christian people to react angrily. When you lose your temper and retaliate, that puts you right down on his level. The cameras are there to catch it; the newspapers report it; people see it. Abraham Lincoln was urged to respond to an accusation against his administration. He said, "I wish no explanation made to my enemies. What they want is a squabble and a fuss, and they can have it if we explain. They can't if we don't." Your resistance may produce a fight, and that's to the advantage of the adversary. "In your anger, do not sin" (Ephesians 4:26). Christ wants to present us "without blemish and free from accusation" (Colossians 1:22). Don't retaliate; just go on.

When Nehemiah was rebuilding the walls of Jerusalem, it was happening so fast the critics were really angry. They sent a letter to Nehemiah that said, "Would you stop working and come on down and have a meeting? We've got some things we want to talk to you about."

Nehemiah said, "I'm doing a great work and I can't come down." He just kept building the wall. The critics got even angrier, but the wall got built.

When Plato was falsely accused, an aide frantically asked, "What should we do?" Plato responded, "Live in such a way that all men will know that the charge was false."

## Concentrate on Character

Our primary focus should not be on what we're going to do, but on who we're going to be. We're inclined to concentrate on programs. We want a definite strategy for the future, we want to know the details. But if we develop character, both individually and as a church, then God will unfold His program for us. If we lose our character and our integrity, we're going to fail regardless of how detailed our strategy.

That's what Paul is talking to Titus about when he says, "In your teaching, show integrity." I don't care what field you're in, integrity gets tough sometimes. I heard about a preacher who was given a pie by a woman who was a terrible cook. He took the pie home. His family had tasted her wares before so they just took the pie and threw it outside in the garbage can.

The next Sunday, sure enough, the preacher ran into that woman "How'd you like the pie?" she asked.

He said, "Mrs. Adams, a pie like that really doesn't last very long around our house."

I don't care whether you're a preacher or a plumber or a physician, at times it's tough to practice integrity. But if the church of the future is going to be God's church, we've got to be honest in all things.

*Christianity Today* reported that amid all the scandals, Billy Graham has remained America's most admired religious leader. When asked how he avoided the sexual and financial scandals that had plagued other ministries, Billy Graham replied, "I decided that there were three areas that Satan would attack me in: pride, morals, and finances. Over the years, I've tried to set up safeguards against the dangers of each. From the earliest days, I've never had a meal alone with a woman other than my wife, Ruth. I've never traveled in a car alone with a woman other than my wife." *Christianity Today* reported that Billy Graham gets a straight salary from his organization that amounts to about $70,000 a year. He accepts no speaker's fees. He's given away all the royalties on his books. He's said from the beginning, "I was frightened and I still am that I could do something that would dishonor the Lord."

Because you're part of the church, people examine your life more closely. Nobody expects you to be perfect, but you do need to practice authenticity and integrity. Our message means nothing if there's not a legitimate lifestyle behind it.

In your life, Paul says, demonstrate seriousness. Now, being serious doesn't mean that we can never laugh or that we have to be always somber about life. Jesus often used humor. The Bible says, "A cheerful heart is good medicine" (Proverbs 17:22). What it means is that we're not frivolous. We never leave the impression that we're only here to have a good time. If all that happens when people come to church is that they have a good laugh, we've failed—because we are talking about life and death matters here. Humor is a serious part of what we're doing. But our goal is to honor Jesus Christ, to go to Heaven when we die, and take as many people as we can with us—and that's no joke. Our seriousness is not demonstrated by whether we laugh or not, but by our sacrifice and our intensity.

"In your teaching show soundness of speech that cannot be condemned" (vv. 7, 8). Christianity is based on fact. It makes good common sense and it should be presented logically. One of the problems with churches today is that we try to present the message only in emotional terms and the world is seeking intelligent answers.

People ask two kinds of questions, emotional questions or intellectual questions. We should never respond to an emotional question with an intellectual answer or vice-versa. If someone is broken-hearted because a loved one has died, and they ask, "How could God do this to me?", don't give them a long, theological intellectual answer about all the reasons that this happens. You just need to put your arm around them and say, "I don't know, but I know in my heart you're going to see that loved one again some day."

But if a person asks an intellectual question about the validity of the Bible or the reality of the resurrection, they don't just need emotional answers. "Well, I know Jesus lived because my grandmother was such a good person, and I know I'm going to see her someday." That comes across as shallow. That's the time to talk about the proof of the resurrection. That's the time to talk about the prophecies of the Bible and the reality of God's Word.

In order to meet the challenges of the future, the church has to do more than measure its effectiveness by whether people are emotionally charged or not. We'd better be ready for intellectual challenges. We'd better be ready to present the gospel in such sound a way that people can't refute it. *The Living Bible* paraphrases verse 8 like this: "Your conversation should be so sensible and logical that anyone who wants to argue will be ashamed of himself because there won't be anything to criticize in anything you say."

"Always be prepared to give an answer to everyone who asks you to give a reason for the hope that you have. But do this with gentleness and respect" (1 Peter 3:15). Give an intellectual answer for the reason for your hope, but don't do it arrogantly.

Our world has lost its way morally and spiritually. The

average person on the street knows that we're losing our common sense. What a prime time for us to come with the legitimacy of the gospel. The simple truth of the Bible is powerful, and it makes much common sense. Jesus said, "The one who hears these words of mine and obeys them will be like a wise man who builds his house on a rock." Nothing will inspire future generations to faithfulness more than a consistent demonstration of genuine Christianity coupled with some sound biblical, intellectual reasons for believing. God will take care of the future if we're just obedient today.

Dr. Olin Hay used to tell about an old janitor at the Baptist seminary who would sit in the bleachers and wait for the young men to finish practicing basketball so he could lock up. Often he would sit with a Bible in his lap and read. One evening some of the young men asked him what he was reading and he said he was reading the book of Revelation, and they began to tease him, saying, "Well, do you understand that book? Do you know what's going to happen?"

"Well, I don't understand it all," the old man said, "but I know this one thing this book teaches me."

"What's that?" they asked.

He said, "Jesus is going to win!"

The victory for the church is assured in Jesus Christ, and when you are aware of the conclusion of the story, you don't need to worry a lot about the development of the plot. One day Jesus Christ is going to return for the church. The Bible says He's going to put all of His enemies under His feet. Even the most arrogant tongue is going to confess that Jesus is Lord and the most flagrant disbeliever is going to bow the knee before Him. That's the ultimate future of the church.

Until that day comes, let's faithfully pass on the baton to younger generations. Let's not retaliate when some accuse falsely. Let's practice integrity and honesty. Then when the future comes to its climax, we'll be found on the victor's side.

# Make Christianity Attractive in the Marketplace

## Titus 2:9-10

IMAGINE THAT YOUR favorite football team is in a huddle. They're behind by one point with ten seconds to go and the ball is on the five yard line; they're just about ready to score. The fans in the stadium are on their feet. They know the next play is crucial. But, the team just stays in the huddle and talks. The referee blows the whistle, throws a flag, and steps off a five-yard penalty for delay of game. But the team still stays in the huddle, holding hands and talking. Finally, they burst out of the huddle cheering. They run to the sidelines and out of the stadium, get in their cars, and go home.

Every fan would be frustrated and angry with that kind of action, because a huddle is not an end in itself. The purpose of the huddle is to plan the strategy for the next play and to encourage those who are participating. A team would never just huddle and then hurry home.

But sometimes that's an accurate portrayal of the church. Once a week we gather for worship. Christians should worship—that's a special time. But the problem is that some of us see this gathering as an end in itself. We measure the church's effectiveness by the number of people in the holy huddle and by the inspiration of the hour, and then we disperse and disappear until next week. But there's a spiritual conflict going on in the world. Worship is a time for us to be inspired and to receive instruction on how to make an impact for Jesus Christ in everyday society.

Jesus said, "You are the salt of the earth. But if the salt loses its saltiness, how can it be made salty again? It is no longer good for anything, except to be thrown out and trampled by men" (Matthew 5:13). The purpose of salt is to add flavor, and it has to penetrate the meat to do that. The purpose of the church is to make a difference in the world, but we have to penetrate the world in order to accomplish that. The effectiveness of the church is not measured by what goes on in worship service, but by what goes on in the lives of its people throughout the week.

Paul discusses this basic truth in Titus 2:9, 10. If we can grasp the three principles he presents, it will make a big difference in how we view the church and our everyday responsibilities.

## Christianity Is to Permeate Every Area of Life

*Time* magazine is divided into several different categories. There's a segment about Sports, and one about Business, one about Art, one about Entertainment, and usually toward the back there's a section about Religion. That's the way many people want to segment life. They want to isolate religion from everyday life.

Educators say, "Moral values are to be taught in the home, spiritual values ought to be taught in the church, but we are in the business of education, teaching facts in the school. We have a value-free sex education program, because it's not our job to teach spiritual values."

Politicians say, "I am personally against abortion, but I will not try to impose my religious values on the American people. I think that's a private matter. People ought to be free to choose whatever they want."

Businessmen say, "That's fine if you go to church, that's good, but don't try to mix business and religion, or religious ethics will cause you to lose your shirt every time."

The ACLU says, "It's OK to celebrate Christmas in the home and in the church, but when you begin to put a manger scene on the grounds of the state capitol, that's mixing the state and religion, and we can't have that."

People in the world don't mind if we meet in a huddle and talk. But they don't want our faith to permeate other areas of life. In all honesty, many Christians would prefer it that way, too. Just come for an hour of inspiration on Sunday morning and then do as you please the rest of the week. But the Lord Jesus Christ intended for our faith to dominate every facet of our lives. The Bible says, "Whatever you do, whether in word or deed, do it all in the name of the Lord Jesus" (Colossians 3:17).

Christ is "the head of the body, the church; . . . so that in everything He might have the supremacy" (Colossians 1:18). Paul talks about being subject in everything, so that in every way we will represent Christ properly. *Everything!* When you accept Jesus Christ as your personal Savior, you also accept Him as Lord. He's not just the Lord for one hour of praise on Sunday morning. He's the Lord of all. He wants to be honored on Sunday morning, but He also wants to be honored in your entertainment life, in your school life, in your date life, in your occupation, in your business.

Understand what is expected of you when you become a member of the church. You are not expected just to attend services regularly, and give a little of your money, and invite your neighbor if you think the program is going to be good. You're expected to make Jesus Christ Lord of everything. That doesn't mean perfection, but it does mean the appropriation of His Word. It does mean that you acknowledge the authority of Jesus Christ in every facet of your existence.

Christianity is a new way of thinking, feeling, and behaving about everything. Because if it is true that God created us, then He's Lord of everything. If it is true that Jesus Christ died to save us from our sins and from Hell, then that message is needed by everyone. If it is true that Christ rose from the dead and promises perfect, eternal life to those who abide in Him, then that hope should dominate our lives every day.

Let's say you work as a cook in a restaurant. One day a fire breaks out in the kitchen, and you can see that it's out of control. Out in the dining room, everybody is relaxed and having a good time. But if you see the situation and you care about people, you're forced to go out and interrupt them. You're going to go out and say, "Ladies and gentlemen, may I have your attention, please?" Now, momentarily, you're going to be conspicuous and maybe resented because the people eating don't want to have their meals interrupted, the waiters don't want to miss out on their tips, and the owner doesn't want the establishment to have a negative image. But you will risk that moment of being resented if you believe you have a message that will save those people's lives.

The same is true with Christianity. It affects everything and everybody if it is true. That's why when the early Christians were told not to preach any more in the name of the Lord Jesus in the streets of Jerusalem, they said, "We can't help but speak about what we've seen and heard." No area of life should be unaffected by Jesus Christ. The world may not like that idea, but that's the truth. In everything, Christ is to have supremacy. We're to be His representatives every minute, every place.

Allan Dunbar is the colorful minister of a church in Calgary, Canada, and he has a television program that is seen on cable throughout Canada. A lot of people recognize him. Once he was flying to Phoenix, Arizona, and his plane stopped in Las Vegas for about 50 minutes. He didn't just want to sit on the plane since he'd never been to Las Vegas before, so he got out and walked through the airport.

A lot of slot machines were there, the one-armed bandits. He had two quarters in his pocket. He thought, "I'm hundreds of miles from home. Nobody will recognize me here, and there aren't very many people." So he slipped the two quarters into the slot machine and pulled the arm.

Quarters came pouring out from everywhere, clanging in that tray. He gathered them up, stuffed them into his pockets and carried them back onto the plane. He'd made $28.00 on those two quarters, so he was just delighted.

When he landed in Phoenix and he was walking through the airport, a couple called out to him and he went to meet them. "Pastor Dunbar," they said, "we watch you on television in Canada every week. We respect the Word that you preach. You're really a man of God. We're here on vacation in Phoenix, and we're waiting to meet our son, who's on the same plane you're on."

When the boy came, they introduced him to Pastor Dunbar. "Oh yes, Reverend," he said. "How much did you make back there in Las Vegas?"

We have to have a guard up all the time. Our faith is to permeate everything we do, every place we go. Our home life, our church life, our jobs, even our entertainment. That may seem like a heavy responsibility, and it is, but in everything He is to have supremacy.

## Our Responsibility Is to Attract Others to Christ

"Make the teaching about God our Savior attractive" (v. 10). Kenneth West, in his word study, says the Greek word means to "adorn like a cosmetic." In other words, our lifestyle is to be a cosmetic that enhances the gospel. The world's stereotype of a Christian is somebody who never has a good time and tries to prevent other people from having a good time. Sometimes our attitude and our countenance justify that kind of conclusion. I know some people who seem to be pretty happy in church, but when they go out into the world and associate with people who are not Christian, they are so insecure they either clam up completely or they don't seem to enjoy themselves at all. If they ever approach a non-Christian about their faith, they are often so defensive that they come across as angry and condemning. Rebecca Pippert, in her book, *Out of the Salt-shaker*, wrote, "Christians and non-Christians have something in common. We're both uptight about evangelism. Our fear as Christians seems to be, 'How many people did I offend this week?' We think we must be a little obnoxious in order to be good evangelists."

The Lord is represented in a pretty unattractive way in some circles. The Bible does say that there was "no comeliness about him" (Isaiah 53:2). But we need to remember that Jesus Christ had a charisma that attracted people. He drew people to himself by the thousands. Now the common artist's portrayal of Jesus doesn't make Him look very attractive. He looks like He's sad, and His countenance is weak, almost effeminate. He has long matted hair. He looks as if He just got out of the hospital or something. That picture doesn't attract anybody. I think we need to erase that image from our minds.

He was a strong man physically. He was a carpenter. The carpenters in that day had to fell their own trees. He was a lumberjack. His hands would be calloused; his shoulders would be broad. He associated with fishermen. His face would be bronzed by the sun. He was a caring person emotionally. He knew how to weep and to laugh, and people who had troubles could bring their problems to Jesus and He understood. He was a courageous person publicly. He was not afraid to take a stand that was against the tide of popular opinion. He was a brilliant man intellectually, He had no peer. Even His enemies were amazed at the depth of His insight. They said, "How can this be? He never went to our schools." He was an excellent communicator. The common people heard Him gladly, and the lawyers and the doctors were amazed at His teaching. Never a man spoke like this man.

People from every walk of life were attracted to Jesus. There was the blind beggar Bartimeus, who called out from the road near Jericho, "Son of David, have mercy on me." There was the aristocrat, Nicodemus, who sneaked an audience with Jesus at night. There was that wicked woman at the well, married five times and living with a man to whom she was not married. She went to the city and said, "Come see a man who told everything about me, and yet he still cares for me." There was the pious, rich young ruler who asked Jesus, "I've kept the law, what do I lack yet?" Little children wanted to sit on His lap, older people wanted to be healed by Him. Crowds of more than 5,000 people would go out into the wilderness and follow Him around the lake just to hear Him speak.

Just before He died, Jesus comforted His disciples by saying, "Peace I leave with you; my peace I give you," and "As I have loved you, so you must love one another" (John 14:27; 13:34). We're to represent Christ in the world. That means there should be an attractiveness about us. There ought to be a peace, there ought to be a joy, there ought to be a love and a vitality that makes other people look at us and say, "I want to know the same Lord they know. They've got something I don't have."

Pat Boone is someone who does that well. He's an entertainer and an outspoken Christian, and it seems to me that he represents the Lord in an attractive way. He was in town for the Foster Brooks Pro-Celebrity Golf Tournament, and at the program that night, the emcee, Gordie Tapp, told one raunchy story after another. Finally, it got time for Pat Boone to sing a couple of songs. He said, "You know, I came to this tournament because Foster Brooks came to my tournament in Chattanooga, where the proceeds go to a Christian orphanage. Foster asked me if he could tell a particular joke that night, and I said, 'Well, Foster, that's funny, but that's probably not appropriate for this Christian audience.' Then Foster asked about a second joke, and I said, 'Foster, that's funny too, but you better not tell that one either.' By the time Foster got done screening his jokes, he only had about three minutes of material left." Then Pat Boone turned to Gordie Tapp, the emcee. He said, "Gordie, if you'd been there, you'd have had to do a mime act!" I thought it was just about the best line of the night, and the audience appreciated it too.

Other people should be able to see that we have a good time. They should see an attractiveness about us that draws them to Jesus Christ. Jesus said, "Let your light shine before men, that they might see your good deeds and praise your

Father in heaven" (Matthew 5:16). We're not supposed to turn people off.

## Our Job Presents Our Primary Opportunity for Witness

Paul says, "Teach slaves to be subject to their masters" (v. 9). None of us is a slave, but most of us are employed by someone. The principles set forth in this passage are applicable to us all. Paul told the slaves to perform their jobs in such a way that they'll be magnets attracting people to Christ. Christianity is to make a difference in how you perform your work. In fact, from a spiritual perspective, the primary purpose of your job is not just to earn a living, but to be a witness to Jesus Christ. There are going to be non-Christians around you, and weak Christians who need to be reinforced.

When John Kennedy was campaigning for the presidency in the late 50's, he visited a coal mine in West Virginia. One coal miner said, "Mr. Kennedy, is it true that you're the son of one of the wealthiest men in America?"

Kennedy said, "Yes, it is."

He said, "Mr. Kennedy, is it true that you've never really wanted for anything in your life?"

John Kennedy said, "Well, I guess so."

He said, "Mr. Kennedy, is it true that you've never done a hard day's work in all of your life?"

Kennedy nodded.

The coal miner said, "Mr. Kennedy, I want to tell you something, sir—you haven't missed a thing."

Maybe that's the way you see your job—a kind of drudgery you put up with. You'd get out of it if you could. But, God sees your job as an opportunity for you to introduce Jesus Christ to those who don't know Him, and to try to encourage and reaffirm those who do.

Robert Mattox, in his book, *The Christian Employee*, suggests that God arranges our lives so that we have to work with non-Christians. He says we average 36% of our waking hours at work, and we complain about the worldly people we have to work with and say we would never associate with those people in any other setting. But God has arranged it so that the Christian life interacts at work with people we would probably avoid otherwise. A lot of Christian people think that if they really got spiritual, they would quit their secular work and become missionaries. God does call some people into full-time church work, but the truth is, He probably has you working where He wants you right now. You have to interact with people who need the contact of the gospel. They would not listen to a preacher; they would not read a tract; but they do observe your life—and you have the opportunity to get to know them and influence them.

*The Wall Street Journal* reported on a survey of 750 non-church businessmen who were asked, "With whom would you like to discuss spiritual things: A member of your family, a clergyman, a missionary, or a fellow businessman?" Ninety percent of them said they preferred to talk to a fellow businessman. It's not paid representatives that people believe, it's satisfied customers. Your job is an opportunity for you to be a missionary.

It's important that it be done properly, and Paul gives some suggestions here. He says, "Teach slaves to be subject to their masters in everything" (v. 9). Teach them to have a submissive spirit. That doesn't come naturally. From infancy we exhibit a rebellious spirit. On most jobs, if people are told to be in at 8:00, they'll bump up against the rules and see if they can be there at 8:05 and get by with it. If they can be there at 8:05, it'll be 8:10. If they're given three additional sick days for the year, they'll find some way to get sick and take those personal days.

One business attempted to establish a drug testing program for its employees working in sensitive areas. The employees immediately filed a grievance with the National Labor Relations Board. They said, "We don't take drugs, but we don't want the company infringing on our rights and telling us what to do." There's something in our spirit that tries to step across the line of authority.

Christians are to have a compliant spirit at work, learn to

repress pride, and respect delegated authority. Christian slaves were told to be obedient to their masters—even, the Bible says, masters who were harsh and unreasonable. How much more should we, if we voluntarily take a position, have a submissive spirit toward those in authority over us? Even if we don't fully understand why the directives are given.

Reggie Jackson, then playing for Baltimore, was on first base. He waited for the signal to steal because he knew that he could get a jump on the pitcher and beat the catcher's throw. Earl Weaver, the manager, had told his players not to steal unless he gave them the signal. No signal was given but Jackson, knowing that he could make it, took off anyway. He easily slid into second base safely. He got up and dusted off his uniform and smugly looked over at the dugout because he knew that his safe steal had vindicated his judgment. But after the game, manager Weaver took him aside and explained why he hadn't given the steal signal. The next batter was Lee May, the most powerful hitter they had, next to Jackson. Since first base was now open, they intentionally walked May, negating his bat. The next batter was one who had been ineffective against that particular pitcher, and Weaver felt that he had to pinch hit early in the game, weakening his defense and his bench. The Orioles went on to lose the game.

You see the problem? Jackson had a limited perspective. He had a handle on pitchers and catchers, but that's the only thing he saw. Weaver was watching the whole game. He had a larger perspective. Jackson wanted to steal second base. Weaver wanted to win the ball game.

At times you might think you know more than your boss, and perhaps you do. But perhaps he or she sees the bigger picture. It's not your task to second guess, but to be submissive. The people you work with can tell whether you are proud and rebellious or whether you are humble and cooperative. One of our teenage boys once brought a couple of school teachers and a school administrator to church. They were so impressed with his polite spirit and submissive attitude in school, they respected his request to come to church. If he had been defiant in school, they would never have come.

The "nobody tells me what to do" attitude doesn't belong in the life of the Christian. The way we respond to authority says a lot about our submission to the authority of Christ. The Bible says that Jesus humbled himself and became obedient even to death.

Paul tells Titus to teach slaves to try to please their masters, or in other words, to have a pleasant spirit. Sometimes we're afraid that if we try to please those who are superior to us, we'll be accused of being a brown-noser. We bend over backward not to do that. This is because we want to please our peers, and ultimately, we want to please ourselves. Paul says slaves should try to please their masters. Notice he says, "try." Some superiors can never be pleased. But as much as possible, try to be cooperative. Make your employer look good. Ours is not to be a grudging obedience that grumbles behind the back of the boss. We're to obey pleasantly and willingly. That means we smile; we have an upbeat spirit. It means we try to do our best all the time.

An article in *Campus Life* magazine called, "Lady in 415," told of a nurse who sought to be pleasant on the job.

"Eilene was one of her first patients. She was totally helpless. A cerebral aneurysm had left her with no conscious control over her body. As near as doctors could tell, Eilene was totally unconscious, unable to feel pain and unaware of anything going on around her. It was the job of the hospital staff to turn her over every hour to prevent bedsores, and to feed her twice a day what looked like a thin mush through a stomach tube.

"Caring for her was a thankless task, the nurse wrote. 'When it's this bad,' an older student nurse had told her, 'you have to detach yourself emotionally from the whole situation. Otherwise, you just throw up every time you walk into her room.' As a result, more and more, she came to be treated as a thing, a vegetable. The hospital jokes about her room were gross and dehumanizing. But the young student nurse decided that she couldn't treat this person like the others had treated her. She talked to Eilene, sang to her, encouraged her, and even brought her little gifts.

"One day, when things were especially difficult, and it would have been easy for the young nurse to take out her frustrations on the patient, she was especially kind. It was Thanksgiving Day and the nurse said to the patient, 'I was in a cruddy mood this morning, Eilene, because it was supposed to be my day off. But now that I'm here, I'm glad. I wouldn't have wanted to miss seeing you on Thanksgiving. Do you know that this is Thanksgiving, Eilene?' Just then the telephone rang, and as the nurse turned to answer it, she looked quickly back at the patient.

"'Suddenly,' she writes, 'Eilene was looking at me, crying. Big, damp circles stained her pillow, and she was shaking all over.' That was the only human emotion that Eilene ever showed any of them, but it was enough to change the whole attitude of the hospital staff toward her.

"Not long afterward, Eilene died. The young nurse closed her story saying, 'I keep thinking about her. It occurred to me that I owe her an awful lot. Except for Eilene, I might never have known what it's like to give myself to someone who can't give it back.'"

"Slaves, obey your earthly masters in everything; and do it not only when their eye is on you and to win their favor, but with sincerity of heart and reverence for the Lord. Whatever you do, work at it with all your heart, as working for the Lord, not for men, since you know that you will receive an inheritance from the Lord as a reward. It is the Lord Christ that you are serving" (Colossians 3:22). You are not just serving a superior, you're serving the ultimate superior, Jesus Christ. He's taking note of how you're performing on the job, so do it pleasantly.

Paul also says, don't talk back to your employer. People talk back to their bosses in all kinds of ways, usually behind their backs. They say, "Look, that's not my job. That's not in my job description. I've been doing this for ten years. I know what I'm doing, so buzz off." Or they can complain, gripe, and moan about how hard they work and make it miserable for everybody. These complainers lose the respect of their fellow employees, even though that attitude may not be expressed outright.

"No man can tame the tongue. It is a restless evil, full of deadly poison" (James 3:8). Learn to control your tongue at work. Don't get involved in all the griping and rumors that are circulating. You can always find somebody to gripe with. There will always be somebody telling you how tough you've got it. But for the most part, you give a good witness for Jesus Christ if you restrain your tongue.

Paul said, have a right attitude toward money. Don't steal from your master. Slaves would especially be tempted to steal since they were so poor. Taking little things that go unnoticed is still a problem today. But it's not just stealing, it's your attitude toward material things that people notice. Are you always griping about being underpaid, and always begging for an increase in salary? Do you get involved in all the conversations around you about what things you want and what you're going to buy? If you're just one of the bunch, then your values shine through. Others ought to be able to see that your attitude is like Paul's: "I know what it is to be in need, and I know what it is to have plenty. I have learned the secret of being content in any and every situation, whether well fed or hungry, whether living in plenty or in want. I can do everything through him who gives me strength" (Philippians 4:12, 13). If you want to open some eyes of the people around you at work, just leave the impression that you're content with what you've got.

Then Paul says, "Show you can be fully trusted." The basic philosophy of the workplace today is not to trust anybody. Security forces begin with the premise that 85% of employees will rip you off if they have the chance. But once again, we're to be distinctive. We're to demonstrate that we can be trusted. We'll do what we're asked to do. We won't rip anybody off.

When Joseph was Potiphar's slave, Potiphar left everything he had in Joseph's care. With Joseph in charge, he did not concern himself with anything except the food that he ate. Joseph was that dependable, that trustworthy. I know that Potiphar was impressed with Joseph's God.

A slave owner once stood examining a slave, a young man who was on the auction block. He looked the slave in the eye and said, "Sir, if I buy you, will you be honest?"

The slave responded, "Sir, I'll be honest whether you buy me or not."

That's integrity, that's trustworthiness. Wherever you are, regardless of who you're with, you're trustworthy.

We don't influence people by carrying a big black Bible to work, having noontime Bible studies, and twisting people's arms, nearly as much as we do by having a submissive, pleasant spirit, restraining the tongue, and being honest and trustworthy.

When people see Jesus Christ in us, they're attracted to Him. So whatever you do, in word or deed, do it all in the name of the Lord Jesus.

# Live Holy Lives in an Unholy World

## Titus 2:11-14

MOSES HAD A tough job. His task was to lead the Hebrew slaves out of Egypt into the land of Canaan. Physically, that was not such a difficult task. It was a distance of only about 350 miles. They could walk that in about three weeks. Besides, God's miraculous power was there to overcome any obstacles in their way. God had brought ten plagues to soften the stubborn heart of Pharaoh so they would be released. God had parted the Red Sea so they would be forever free. God had given them manna to eat every day, and water from a rock. God had given them a pillar of fire at night and a pillar of cloud by day to guide them.

On the surface, then, it appeared that Moses' job would be a piece of cake. But the real problem wasn't the physical move from Egypt to Canaan—it was the spiritual transition that also had to take place. The Hebrew people had been slaves for 400 years. Their intellectual training was minimal. They were not accustomed to thinking through their problems. Their moral values were poor. For four centuries, they had been exposed to the pagan lifestyle of Egypt. They did not have a good grasp on right and wrong. They had limited experience. Their maturity was weak. They had lived from hand to mouth for so long that they were not accustomed to planning for the future and making sound judgments. It's difficult to lead people like that. They were shallow, rebellious, stubborn, impatient, and complaining. Moses was probably anxious to get it over with.

But once they arrived at the promised land in several months, they really weren't ready to occupy that new territory. They didn't have faith in God. They weren't responsible enough to develop a government, build a military, or manage a business. Maturity takes a while to develop. People need time to cope with freedom. It took the children of Israel forty years of wandering in the wilderness before they were ready for the promised land. God wanted them to be a special people, distinctive from the nations around them. God was going to use those Hebrew people to be the ones through whom the Messiah would come into the world. They would have to learn to think, feel, and behave in the way that God did.

God is calling a special people out of the world today —the church. Jesus Christ is our leader. His death on the cross has secured our freedom from the slavery of sin. We've walked through the waters of baptism. We've eaten the manna, the Lord's Supper. We drink of the rock of the Holy Spirit. We have the Bible to guide us every day. We're marching towards Heaven, where we're going to spend eternity with God. But even though we have been saved by Christ, a difficult transition is occurring in our lives. We're to become like God in His holiness. Our salvation occurs immediately when we accept Jesus Christ as our Savior. But what the Bible calls our sanctification is a purifying process that takes place over a period of time.

Christ "gave himself for us to redeem us from all wickedness, and to purify for himself a people that are his very own" (v. 14). But the problem is that we're not separate from the world. We're to be in the world, but not of it. A maturing process must take place in our lives as we become His people. One of the greatest needs of today is for Christian people to understand their role—to live holy lives in a world that has gone wrong.

## Difficult Instructions

In Titus 2:11-14 we receive instructions, incentives, and the ingredients necessary for us to live as the people of God in the midst of a pagan society. The instruction is difficult to follow. It says that the grace of God "teaches us to say 'No' to ungodliness and worldly passions" (v. 12) The worldly passions that we are to resist can be divided into three categories. The Bible calls them, "the lust of the flesh, the lust of the eyes, and the pride of life." We could label them worldly pleasure, material possessions, and human pride. Those three passions beat within the heart of every human being, and if uncontrolled, will eventually enslave us in demanding habits. It is difficult to say no to those things because everything about this present age is designed to stimulate worldly desire.

This present age is expert at stimulating sexual passion. Video stores have erotic movies for rent. Billboards catch your eye with provocative pictures. The television camera in an advertisement for a diet drink has a close-up scanning of a near-naked body. It is difficult if you're a red-blooded American male or female to say 'no' day after day to such skillful attempts at the arousal of the flesh. A foreign churchman visiting America quipped, "Every day in America it is sex o'clock."

This present age is an expert at inflaming a passion for material possessions, too. In a golf tournament I participated in, each par three had a brand new automobile sitting right beside the tee. All I had to do to win that car was to hit that tiny ball in that great big hole about 160 yards away. Just looking at that car, my hands would start to tremble and I'd get a choking in my throat. I would pray, "Lord, if I win that car, I'll just use it to visit old ladies in the hospital, nothing else." I had three chances. I didn't come within 50 yards of the green on any of them.

Everywhere you go today, you can find stimulation for more things. The lottery says, "Just a little money and you win big." Homarama says, "You can have this kind of home." Advertisements say, "You can have this dream vacation." We are a materialistic culture. Patrick Henry's cry was, "Give me liberty or give me death!" A few generations later, we weakened to just "Give me liberty." Today our cry is just, "Give me. Give me."

This present age is also expert in inflaming status-consciousness. We have to wear designer jeans, carry Gucci pocketbooks, and drive the right model car. We think it's demeaning to use generic brands, even though they may be just as good. We spend money we don't have to buy things we don't need to impress people we don't like. Garry Trudeau, author of the *Doonesbury* cartoon strip, said in a commencement address at Colgate University, "We live in a world where we would rather be envied than esteemed. And when we reach that place," he added, "may God help us."

We're to be the people of God. We're to say no to worldly passions no matter how attractive they may be at the moment, and that's not easy.

Jesus Christ did. Satan came to Him and said, "You're hungry, Jesus. Why don't you turn these stones into bread and then eat it? Just satisfy your physical appetite."

Jesus said, "No, it's written, 'Man doesn't live by bread alone.' There's something more important than just doing what feels good."

Then Satan took Him to a high hill and showed Him all the kingdoms of the world in an instant and said, "If you'll just bow down and worship me, I'll give you all these things."

Jesus said, "No, it's written, 'Worship God only, not things.'"

Then Satan took Him to the pinnacle of the temple and said, "If you'll just jump off, it's written in the Bible that the angels will catch you. What a spectacular stunt that would be! People would come out to see that. You could be famous, Jesus."

But Jesus said, "No, it's written, 'Don't put the Lord your God to the test.'"

Jesus said no to physical pleasure, material possessions, and worldly power. He is proof that it can be done.

Living holy lives in this world can be a difficult assignment, not only because we're supposed to say no to temptation, but because we're supposed to say yes to godliness. We're to "live self-controlled, upright and godly lives in this present age" (v. 12). We're to be controlled by reason, not by passion, and do that which is right.

If you're trying to improve your body, it's one thing to say no to chocolate sundaes. It's something else to say yes to aerobics and exercise. We just can't go around saying no to the passions of this world and leave ourselves in a vacuum. We've got to say yes to positive living.

We're to be "eager to do what is good" (v. 14). *The Living Bible* paraphrases that, "We're to have a real enthusiasm for doing kind things for others." We're to be enthusiastic about worshiping, loving people, developing our families, and being honest on the job. Jesus was. He said no to the pleasures of this world, and then He went about doing good—healing the sick, ministering to the needy, teaching the truth. In fact the Bible says, "Who for the joy that was set before him endured the cross." He was eager to forgive sin.

As part of the "Just Say No" campaign, in the hope of developing a drug-free America, President Reagan appointed several aides to speak to high school assemblies to encourage young people to say no to drugs. One of his aides went to the largest high school in the Bronx. He spoke for 45 minutes to 3,000 young people. At the end of his speech, he said, "I would like a volunteer." He selected a young man who appeared to be a senior in high school and brought him up front.

He said, "Now, young man, what I would like for you to do is take off all of your clothes in front of these kids."

The boy said, "No way. I'm not going to do that."

The man said, "You've forgotten who I am. I'm an aide to the President of the United States. I'm very close to him. I could get on the phone right now and have him command you to take off all your clothes."

The boy said, "You can get the President to call, but I'm not going to do that in front of these kids."

"Oh," the aide said, "I understand what you want. You want money." He took out his wallet and he handed him a twenty dollar bill. "Now, for this twenty dollars, would you take off your clothes?"

The boy said, "No! You could hand me a hundred dollar bill, but I'm not going to do it!"

The speaker then turned to the kids and said, "Would you like to see this boy take his clothes off?"

The kids began chanting, "Take your clothes off. Take your clothes off."

The boy said, "They can chant all day long. I'm not going to do it."

Then the speaker made his point. "I want you to understand what you've just done. You've said no to something stupid. You've said no to power. You've said no to money, and you've said no to your peers. If you can say no in here, you can do it out there. Go say no to drugs." He sat down to thunderous applause.

When you go to church on Sunday morning, at least for a time you say no to worldly passions and yes to doing something good. If you can do it in church, you can do it out there. "No temptation has seized you but what is common to man" (1 Corinthians 10:13), meaning Jesus Christ. God is faithful. He will not let you be tempted beyond what you can bear. When you are tempted, He'll provide a way out so that you can bear up under it.

## Powerful Incentives

Paul gives us three powerful incentives to live up to in this passage. First he says, "Remember God's grace." This has to do with Christ's death on the cross. "The grace of God that brings salvation has appeared to all men" (v. 11). He's talking about the coming of Jesus Christ into the world. Jesus came to bring salvation. Jesus did not come into this world for the primary purpose of saying, "Remember there's a God in Heaven," or "be kind one to another." Jesus came into this world for the express purpose to die on the cross for our sins. He "gave himself for us to redeem us from all wickedness" (v. 14). To buy us back. That's the reason He came into the world. When Jesus died on that cross, the Bible says, God took all of our sins and laid them on Him. He who knew no sin became sin for us.

Jesus was God in the flesh. When He died, He was not limited by time and space. He died not only for the sins of the past, but for all the sins of all time. He could look down to this year and say, "Bob Russell, I see you when you're born in 1943, I see all the sins that you have committed up to now. I see the life that you live and the sins you commit in the future, and I see the day you die. I'm going to die here, taking the burden of your sins on Me."

Here is an awesome thought: If I sin tomorrow, I add to the burden of Jesus' guilt on the cross, 2000 years ago. I do not fully understand that, but I believe that's what the Bible teaches. "When we Christian people fall away, we crucify the Son of God all over again, and we subject Him to public disgrace" (Hebrews 6:6). Remember the words to that song,

Was it for crimes that I have done,
  He groaned upon the tree?
Amazing pity, grace unknown
  and love beyond degree.

Romans 6:1 is paraphrased in *The Living Bible* like this: "Well, then, should we keep on sinning so that God can keep on showing us more and more kindness and forgiveness? Of course not. Should we keep on sinning when we don't have to? For sin's power over us was broken when we became Christians and were baptized to become a part of Jesus Christ." Remember God's grace. That's a motivation.

The second incentive to holy living comes when we understand God's purpose. It has to do with the present. It's God's purpose "to purify for himself a people that are his very own" (v. 14). In the Old Testament, the Jews were to live distinctively among the heathen nations so that people could say, "Jehovah is the real God." Now we're to go out in the world and live distinctively pure lives, so that people will say "Jesus Christ is still alive."

I once saw a man on the beach who had to weigh over 300 pounds. His T-shirt read, "I conquered anorexia." What a living testimony! Nobody would deny it. People ought to see us in such a way that they can't deny the Lord has been working on us. When they see a loving marriage and disciplined children, honesty on the job, a joyful spirit, and kindness to others, they ought to say, "It's true. Jesus Christ is alive in those people." A clean life is a rebuke to a soiled society. So one of the incentives for living rightly is to remember that you are a part of God's people who are to represent Him in the world.

A third incentive to living holy lives is to believe God's promise for the future: "while we wait for the blessed hope—the glorious appearing of our great God and Savior, Jesus Christ" (v. 13).

When Fayette County officials learned that the Queen of England was going to come to Lexington, Kentucky, they went to work to make sure the airport was clean, the litter was off the highways, and the grass was mowed. One farm outside of Lexington planted all new trees and shrubs and flowers. She wasn't coming to that farm, but she was driving by, and they wanted to make sure it looked nice. When we understand that one day the Lord Jesus Christ is going to return to us, we begin to beautify our lives.

He promised, "I will come again." But we could be lulled to sleep by the present events in this world. Isn't this strange, Russia disarming, all of Eastern Europe turning toward democracy? The Bible says, "There will be a time when people call, 'peace, peace,' when there is no peace." Jesus said, "Be alert, I'll come at an hour when you think not."

The first time He came unaware to people. The next time He's going to come more dramatically; every eye will see Him. The first time He came in meekness. The next time He's going to come in authority; every knee will bow. The first time He came in love. The next time He's going to come in power; all His enemies will be put under His feet.

In Joel 2:31, the Bible talks about the end of the world, and it speaks of "the great and dreadful day of the Lord. But the strange thing is in Acts 2, when Peter preaches the first gospel sermon, he quotes Joel 2 verbatim, except he calls it, "the great and glorious day of the Lord." Whether that's a dreadful day or whether it's a glorious day will depend on your relationship to Jesus Christ. You'll either be under His wrath or under His grace. If we're not under His grace, it's going to be a dreadful day. We need to purify our lives because the Lord is going to return one day.

Years ago I preached a series of four sermons on the second coming. On the first Sunday of that series, I looked out and saw a man in the audience who, I knew, came from a worldly background. He hadn't been in church in years. I thought, "I'm not sure I have anything to say to him that will touch his life where he needs to be touched." But he came back the next Sunday, and the next Sunday. I talked about the timing, the purpose, and the signs of the Lord's coming.

Later he became a Christian. He told me, "That series of sermons on the second coming really put the fear of God into me." It's an awesome thing to realize that one day Christ is going to come in power, judgment, and glory—and we're going to face Him.

"Since everything will be destroyed, . . . what kind of people ought you to be? You ought to live holy and godly lives as you look forward to the day of God and speed its coming" (2 Peter 3:11, 12). How are we going to do this?

## Essential Ingredients

Number one, we're going to have to think. "The grace of God . . . teaches us" (vv. 11, 12). We're told repeatedly in the Bible that Christians are to use their minds. Christ is the teacher; we're the disciples, which means learners. We're to love God with all of our minds. We're to be transformed by the renewing of our minds. We're to have the mind of Jesus Christ in us. Right thinking leads to right behavior and then right feeling. Our world is not accustomed to thinking very much right now. The world is primarily responding by instinct, passion, and emotion. Many people let others do their thinking for them, like educators or the media. As a result, there is a lot of confusion and chaos.

I heard about a second-string quarterback who didn't get into one game the whole year long. In the championship game, the final game of the year, with thirty seconds left to go, the first-string quarterback got hurt. The coach didn't want to, but he had no alternative, so he sent this inexperienced, inadequate quarterback into the game. To his surprise, the quarterback, with thirty seconds to go and his team behind by one point, called play number 15. They hadn't used it all year long. Nobody was ready for it, especially the opponents, and it went for a touchdown. They won the game.

In the celebration in the locker room after the game, the coach went to that quarterback. "I've got to apologize to you," he said. "I probably should have put you in sooner. I didn't know you were that smart. What made you think of Play 15? We haven't run it all year long."

The quarterback said, "Well, to be honest with you, Coach, when I got in there I was so nervous I couldn't think of anything. I looked across at the huddle and saw that big tackle with the number 76, and I just added those two numbers together and called Play 15."

"Well, I'm glad you did," the coach said. "But I've got to be honest with you. Seven and six aren't fifteen."

The boy said, "You know, Coach, if I was as smart as you are, we would have lost the game."

Our world isn't doing much thinking. It lucks out on occasion. Not many people want to think deeply about spiritual matters in particular. People say, "Don't bog me down with that Bible stuff! Don't talk to me about spiritual values. That's for church. I don't want to think about theology." But Christians, as the people of God, ought to think. "Do your best to present yourself to God as one approved, a workman who does not need to be ashamed, and who correctly handles the word of truth" (2 Timothy

2:15). We cannot just come in to church once a week for an emotional high.

Billy Graham preaches a sermon called, "Facts, Faith, and Feeling." They need to be in that order. Facts are to be understood, we respond by faith, and then comes feeling. But when we make feeling our ultimate goal, it's going to come up shallow. Charles Colson says that German Christians broke down prior to World War II under the Nazi attack, except those Christians like Bonhoffer and Niebuhr who had fought through their faith and knew where they stood.

A wonderful thing happens when you learn to think and study on your own. You can't get enough of it, because you realize Christianity is not a fairy tale—it's for real, it's true. It gives you a solid foundation. The Bible says, "Faith comes from hearing the message, and the message is heard through the word of Christ" (Romans 10:17).

Christopher Columbus was stranded in Jamaica. He needed supplies and he knew that a lunar eclipse was going to occur the next day. He told the tribal chief, "The God who protects me is going to punish you unless you give me supplies tonight. A vengeance will fall upon you and the moon will lose its light." When the eclipse darkened the sky, Columbus got all the supplies he needed.

In the early 1900's, hundreds of years later, an Englishman tried the same trick on a Sudanese chieftain. The Englishman said, "If you don't follow my orders, vengeance will fall upon you and the moon is going to lose its light."

The chief looked at him and said, "If you mean the lunar eclipse, that's occurring the day after tomorrow."

When we have the basic knowledge of God's truth, we're not going to get sucked into the deceptions of this world. We're able to think it through and see its shallow nature.

The second thing we need to do may be tougher than thinking, and that is, we have to wait: "while we wait for the blessed hope" (v. 13).

Our world is impatient. We want everything right now. We've got instant tea and instant coffee, instant computers and instant banking, instant cameras and push button phones with instant re-dial features. There's a sign in a shop in Pennsylvania that reads, "Antiques Made While You Wait." That's almost as stupid as the one that said, "Ears Pierced While You Wait." (You don't leave them there and pick them up later!)

Some things that are worthwhile don't come instantly. Maturity, character, wisdom, perceptiveness, and holiness do not come quickly. All through the Scriptures, God tells us, be patient for the coming of the Lord; wait on the Lord; they that wait on the Lord shall renew their strength; don't grow weary in doing good, for in due season you will reap a harvest if you don't give up. Yet I find a lot of Christian people who are impatient. They say, "Oh, Lord, my family's falling apart, I'm not very wealthy, my health isn't right, my life's not what it ought to be—where are You? I'm trying to do what is right. I want it now."

But God urges us over and over again to be patient, to wait. Ultimately, He'll win the victory. Sometimes we can do little except to wait and believe.

Glen Wheeler preached for years in Ironton, Ohio. His wife died several years ago. Glen had really depended on his wife; for a while he was almost lost without her. "I miss the little things about her," he said. "After church when I was finished preaching and when everybody had gone, I'd walk to the car with my wife and she'd slip her arm in mine and she'd always say, 'You're a good man, Glen.' Man, I miss hearing that."

"You know what else I miss?" he said. "I miss her cooking." She was a great cook, and Glen's physique was a testimony to that. "The great thing about meals was so many times after we'd eat, she'd come around and pick up the plates and say, 'Keep your fork, Glen.' I'd love to hear that—'Keep your fork, Glen.' That meant something better was coming, and she made great desserts. I miss that.

"Sometimes it's like I can hear the voice of God saying, 'Keep your fork, Glen. Just wait, the best is yet to come. You'll be together. Be patient.'"

They that wait upon the Lord renew their strength. That's a difficult thing to do in a world that's gone so wrong. But we're promised that if we wait, we'll mount up with the wings of an eagle and fly someday.

A Jewish refugee wrote an inscription on a wall outside Cologne, Germany, during World War II: "I believe in the sun, even when it's not shining. I believe in love even when I'm alone. And I believe in God even when He's silent."

# Respect Your Ministers

## Titus 2:15

A MINISTER'S WIFE in a large congregation asked a new member if he was enjoying the church. He said, "Oh, yes, it's great! I love the building, the music is terrific, and the people here have been warm and friendly."

"What about the preaching?" she asked.

"Well," he said, "that's one area I'm disappointed in. I think the preacher is a little dry, he preaches too long, and he really doesn't relate well to my life."

The minister's wife said, "Do you know who I am?"

He said, "No, I don't."

She said, "I'm the minister's wife."

"Oh," he said. "Do you know who I am?"

She said, "No, I don't."

"Good," he said, and he disappeared into the crowd.

The ministry has fallen into disrepute in the last several years. There have always been jokes about the minister's sermons and his sincerity, but the recent moral failures of well-known television evangelists and well-known ministers have compounded the problem. The American people don't hold the ministry in very high esteem any more. Years ago, the minister was "the parson." The person. He was considered to be the person of education and the most well-traveled person in the community. But today, the ministry is not one of the more honored professions.

It's safe to say that more than half of the conflicts that arise in the church involve the preacher's relationship to the congregation. The people in the church complain that he's too dictatorial, or that he's too passive. He's not spiritual enough, or he's not in touch with the real world. He's always changing things, or he's not contemporary. He's too material-istic, or he doesn't represent us well. He's too isolated in the study, he doesn't feed us on Sunday. There's criticism and defensiveness and division.

On the other hand, preachers get upset because the congregation doesn't respect their leadership. These people will not give me any authority, or they expect me to do everything. They won't give me any space, or they don't care. They won't give their money, or they think I can be bought. There's grumbling and discontent.

Once that kind of tension exists between preacher and congregation, Satan has a foothold and the Holy Spirit is quenched. We read in Acts 2 that the disciples were all of one accord in one place. Then came the outpouring of the Holy Spirit and the explosion of evangelism. Harmony is a prerequisite to power in the church. God does not bless a contentious body. That's why Jesus prayed that we would all be united so that the world would believe He is the Savior.

If the church is going to be alive and growing, it's im-perative that there be a mutual understanding of what is expected of the minister. This is not a subject we'll need to deal with very often. But since we are talking about God's message for a growing church, it's better to discuss it to prevent problems in the future, rather than to try to cure them once they're out of control. When I talk about the ministers, I'm not just referring to the preaching pastor, but all of the full-time staff members of the church.

## The Minister's Identity

The identity of "the minister" in Scripture is a little nebulous. Some people would identify him with the New

Testament evangelists. Paul said to Timothy, "Keep your head in all situations, endure hardship, do the work of an evangelist, discharge all the duties of your ministry" (2 Timothy 4:5). God has called some to be pastors and some to be evangelists, says Ephesians 4. An evangelist in the Bible was one who helped in establishing and developing new congregations. He was told to preach the gospel, set the church in order, and appoint elders in every church. The evangelist's ministry was usually brief, and he was concerned primarily with conversion of the lost.

Other Bible students believe the modern minister is the preaching *pastor* of 1 Timothy 5:17, 18, which reads, "The elders," a term that is used interchangeably with pastor: "the elders who direct the affairs of the church well are worthy of double honor, especially those whose work is preaching and teaching. For the Scripture says, 'Do not muzzle the ox while it is treading out the grain,' and 'the worker deserves his wages.'"

In the New Testament pattern, there is a role for a paid pastor whose responsibility is primarily preaching and teaching. He is not the only pastor, he is one of a plurality who are overseers of the church. It has been the stated position of our congregation in its bylaws that the preacher is considered the paid pastor. The elders made it clear from the time I was first called to their ministry that my primary responsibility would be the public preaching and teaching of the Bible. My other responsibilities have varied significantly over the years, but that has been one constant. For 23 years, I have not had to struggle with my primary role or my identity. I've been called to study and to preach the Bible.

When I began 23 years ago, I was the only paid staff member. My wife was a volunteer secretary for eight months. Then as we grew, we needed to have a secretary for two reasons. Number one, the work load had increased, and number two, the elders didn't think it was a good idea to have a divorced minister! It's tough for husbands and wives to work together. Our first staff addition was a part-time secretary. Then I no longer had to write every word of the church paper.

Since that time, we've added a number of office personnel and we now have sixteen full-time ministers. Each one hired has a distinct purpose: music minister, education minister, and so on. Over the last two years, since our explosion of growth, we've hired seven additional full-time ministers. There's been an Activities Minister, with responsibility for the oversight of the Family Life Center and all the fellowship activities; a Shepherding Minister, responsible for caring for the sick and the hurting; an Administrator, in charge of the overseeing of financial and organizational matters; a Program Director, who oversees the worship service, the sound and lights, and all the programming; a Counseling Minister; a Children's Director; a College Minister; a Junior High Minister. Each of these people is called to a specific function. Each of them relieve me of responsibility so I can focus my attention on study and preaching of the Word. Each of them is functioning well, partly because the elders have given clear job descriptions and a sense of identity to those jobs.

The average minister suffers from a kind of vocational amnesia. He doesn't know why he's there and what his primary responsibility is. *Christianity Today* published a survey of 700 ministers who were asked to list six functions of the ministry in order of importance. They listed preaching first, pastoring, counseling, teaching, organizing, and administration. Then they were asked to rate those same six functions as to the actual amount of time they spent performing that role. Administration was first with 26 hours a week, and preaching, which had been first in priority, was last in time with an average of 3-1/2 hours a week.

If a minister doesn't know what his role is, and the congregation doesn't know what his role is, these are grounds for trouble. I heard about a young man who went into a candy store and ordered three boxes of candy—one large, one medium and one small. The owner of the store asked, "Why do you want three boxes?"

113

He said, "I've got my first date with this girl tonight. If it's an average date, I'm going to give her a small box of candy. If it's a good date and she lets me hold her hand, I'm going to give her a medium box. And if she's really warm and she lets me kiss her, I'm going to give her a large box."

He went to the girl's house and ate dinner with the family. When he was asked to have the blessing he prayed, and he prayed, and he prayed. After dinner, the girl went with him for a walk. "I didn't know you were so spiritual," she said.

"I didn't know your father was the owner of the candy store!" he said.

If you're not clear about somebody's role, it can cause all kinds of problems. It's important that the minister understand what his role is and the congregation understand the primary role.

William Enright compares the minister to a director of a symphony. His task is to blend the talents of the various members and produce music to the glory of God in terms of witness and mission. But if the congregation thinks it's the minister's task to play every instrument, he's in trouble. There's no way he can study and preach and coach the ball team and direct the choir and edit the church paper and visit in the hospital and call on new members and counsel married couples and perform weddings and funerals and pray at public functions and be a youth sponsor and administer the budget and fill the baptistery and turn off the lights and lock the doors. He may, in smaller congregations, try to perform all those functions, but he can't do all of them well, and he's vulnerable to criticism. His primary calling is neglected. The church needs to understand we are here to win people to Jesus Christ and then help them to grow. Our minister is here to preach the Word of God in such a way that the lost will be won to Christ and Christians will be motivated to use their gifts for the building up of the church.

## The Minister's Responsibility

The minister's responsibility is threefold, according to this passage. First he is to *teach*. "These are the things you are to teach," Paul said. He admonished Timothy, "Preach the Word, be prepared in season and out of season; correct, rebuke and encourage—with great patience and careful instruction" (2 Timothy 4:2). That means it takes time.

Harry Emerson Fosdick said a minister ought to spend an hour in the study for every minute in the pulpit. When you come to Sunday-school class or you go to church, you ought to learn something about the Bible. That doesn't mean you have to hear something brand new every Lord's Day, something you've never heard before. Maybe it's just a refresher lesson on some of the basics. But we are to be students of the Word, ever learning the truth of God. "The word of God is living and active. Sharper than any double-edged sword, it penetrates even to dividing soul and spirit, joints and marrow, it judges the thoughts and the attitudes of the heart" (Hebrews 4:12).

The Bible has tremendous power when it's taught. That's one reason I usually just go through a book of the Bible when I preach. People will come to me later and say, "Have you been talking to my children? Do you have a pipeline into our home? How'd you know what I was thinking?" When the Bible is taught, it penetrates the thoughts and the attitudes of the heart.

If we ministers are going to teach the Bible, we must do more than relate facts. If you leave church just knowing the size of the ark, that's not going to be helpful to you in everyday life. We have to tell you what the Bible says and show how it applies to you. In his book about preaching called *Between Two Worlds*, John Stott says it's our job to build a bridge between the biblical world and the modern world. Bob Shannon said, "I don't go into the pulpit to explain a passage; I go into the pulpit to meet a need. Now, it just so happens that for every need, there is a passage. When you get the two together, then something happens in preaching."

His responsibility is also to *encourage*. It's easy to get discouraged in our world. You get beat down in your job, the news is depressing, your health's not great, and your family's falling apart; when you come to church, you don't need more bad news. The gospel is good news! Jesus said, "I have come that they may have life, and have it to the full (John 10:10). "For everything that was written in the past was written to teach us, so that through endurance and the encouragement of the Scriptures we might have hope" (Romans 15:4). You shouldn't walk out of church or Sunday school just feeling beat down all the time. David said, "I was glad when they said to me, let's go to the house of the Lord."

Jesus is our model. He was a great teacher. They called Him rabbi, "good teacher." But He was also an encourager. He said, "In this world you will have trouble. But take heart, I have overcome the world" (John 16:33).

I once watched a man who was billed as the greatest teacher of tennis to children. He'd given some of the greatest tennis players their love for the sport. He stood on one side of the net with several dozen balls, and on the other side of the net was a little girl about seven years of age. As he tried to teach her tennis, he was a chatterbox of constant encouragement. "OK, Christine, hold the racket like I told you. That's good, that's great, that's beautiful. Keep it up now." He started hitting balls at her. "Oh, you're doing great!" he said. "I'm proud of you. That's it! Oh, you almost hit that one. Look at that! Hey, that's great! That's the way, way to go! Keep it up. Keep it up." She was just beaming. She began to huff and puff, but she couldn't get enough. He was teaching her to love to play tennis. People respond to encouragement much more than chastisement.

Our task is to give you a love for the Bible, a love for the Lord Jesus Christ, and a love for living. I think people respond much better, and accept criticism much better, if it's balanced with encouragement.

But the minister's responsibility is also to *rebuke*. The Lord said, "Those whom I love, I rebuke and discipline" (Revelation 3:19). Have you ever had somebody tell you that you look terrific all the time? Every time they see you, it's "You look terrific." When you've just gotten out of the hospital, and you know you look lousy—they still say, "You look terrific." Eventually, what they say doesn't mean anything. They've got to tell you the truth for the praise to be worthwhile. The teacher who always praises and affirms, but never disciplines, is going to be in for a long year.

The Christian minister needs to be able to rebuke on occasion, to honestly say, "We're not doing this well." That's hard for me. I don't enjoy saying, "People, when you leave during the invitation hymn, that really is disrespectful because people are making critical decisions, and their decisions are more important than whether you are first in line out of the parking lot, so stay." I don't like to say those things, and people don't like to hear them.

When I was in high school, we had a preacher who was a rebuking specialist. He was a hell fire and brimstone machine. Every Sunday, he would lay us low. He'd shout and holler. For the first couple of sermons, we thought, "This guy is great. He tells it like it is. He convicts you. This is wonderful." But after about two months, we thought, "How long is this guy going to stay?" We'd walk out of there every week with our tails between our legs.

Some people like that kind of preaching. It's a kind of spiritual spanking that salves their conscience. They can say, "Well, we've been punished for our sins this week and now we don't have to do anything about them." But rebuking doesn't have to be very frequent, and it doesn't have to be loud or harsh—in the home, school, or in the church. Rebuking is confronting a problem honestly and motivating change.

Dr. Lewis Foster was a professor of mine in Bible college. Everybody respected him for his intelligence, and he was a great teacher. He hardly ever rebuked. But one day in Bible survey class, he looked down, and in the second row he saw two people playing tic-tac-toe. You didn't do that in his class! Without saying a word, he stopped his lecture and looked at them. They didn't look up; they just kept playing. He walked over and stood by them, and the rest of us felt the hair on the back of our necks standing up from fear.

Suddenly they looked up, and there was the professor looking right down at them. He just said, "Who's winning?"

All you could hear was the whirr of the fan in the room. He looked down for about 15 seconds, walked back up to the platform, picked up his notes and started lecturing. Nobody ever tic-tac-toed in that class again.

The most effective rebukes are not harsh, loud, or condemning. They can be spoken quietly and gently, but the rebuker motivates the "rebukee" to change. Jesus is our model. He could rebuke pretty sternly. He could say, "You scribes and Pharisees, hypocrites! You're like whitewashed tombs, clean on the outside, but inside you're full of dead men's bones." But Jesus could also rebuke gently. When Simon Peter denied Him, Jesus just turned and looked at Peter, and Peter was convicted. Sometimes a spiritual leader has to confront sin and rebuke the offender.

## The Minister's Authority

We're to teach and encourage and rebuke with authority. Where does a minister get his authority? What right do we have to tell anybody what to do? Paul said, "Don't let anybody despise you, make sure they respect you." Our authority does not come from threat of resignation: "If I don't get my way, I'll resign! I'll take my ball and go home."

Authority does not come from a claim of inspiration. "God told me this past week that next month when there's a special offering, everybody is supposed to donate a thousand dollars." (Really, did God tell me that?)

Authority does not come from an attitude of intimidation. Some dictators threaten to humiliate people from the pulpit or belittle them in public.

The minister's authority is based on five sources. First is the call of God. God has gifted some to teach and to preach. If you sense that a person has been gifted that way, called by God to be a minister, you should respect that role.

The second source of authority is the Word of God. The minister's opinions are no more binding on the believer than anyone else's, but if the minister is teaching the Bible, Christians should respect that as authoritative.

The third source of authority is a life of integrity. There's great power in good men or women who live according to the Scripture while they move among the people. But if they sacrifice that integrity, they lose their source of authority.

The fourth is a life of service. Jesus was a servant leader. He didn't lead by imitation, but by example. He washed feet. He ministered to the hurting. He said, "You know that the rulers of the Gentiles lord it over them, and their high officials exercise authority over them. Not so with you. Instead, whoever wants to become great among you must be your servant, and whoever wants to be first must be your slave—just as the Son of Man did not come to be served, but to serve, and to give his life as a ransom for many" (Matthew 20:25-28). The term "minister" signifies a willingness to serve people. So our authority comes not from lording it over others, but trying to serve.

The final source of a minister's authority is the support of the church leaders. God has designated a group of men called elders to be the overseers of the church. The elders are to direct the affairs of the church, and the minister's authority is only as good as the church leaders who stand behind him. There's a formula, R - A = F. Responsibility minus authority equals frustration. If the church leaders undermine his credibility, if they are disrespectful, then the minister has no leverage and he's ineffective. If they stand together, in support of him, then he has authority. If the principal doesn't stand behind the teacher, the teacher has no authority in the classroom. If the board of elders and the deacons don't stand behind the minister, the minister has no authority in the church.

The elders have authority over you only as you are submissive to the will of God. A baseball umpire gets his authority from the commissioner, but if you don't play in the league, he has no authority over you. A foreman at work gets his authority from the owner, but if you don't work at that business, he has no authority over you. A minister of the church gets his authority from the church, but if you're not a Christian or a part of that church, he has no authority over you.

"Obey your leaders and submit to their authority. They keep watch over you as men who must give an account. Obey them so that their work will be a joy, not a burden, for that would be of no advantage to you" (Hebrews 13:17). How can you show respect?

One way you can do it is to have a submissive spirit. If you're asked to do something, be *submissive*. I've been to meetings in which 75 people are sitting in the back of a church building that seats 300 people. Invariably, the preacher will get up and say, "During this first song, let's all move forward and get close down here in front." It's interesting to watch the people's reactions. Half of them come forward and the other half stay put. You can almost see what they're thinking: "You're not going to make me move. This is my pew, this is where I sit." They have a kind of arrogant spirit. The minister stands up there just trembling.

If you're asked to cooperate, if it doesn't violate your convictions, follow instructions. It's a mature Christian who isn't too proud to be submissive, no matter how important they may be in the secular world. If you visit the Family Life Center, and the Director of Activities says just bring two outside guests at a time, then honor that request. If you take your children to the Children's Department and the Children's Director says, "Please don't leave your children unattended, wait until the teacher is here," don't just dump them off, saying that your kids are an exception. If you sing in the choir, or you work in preparation for the worship service, and the director asks you to come ten minutes early, do your best to cooperate.

Second, be *studious*. Don't automatically take everything the preacher says as gospel. Make sure you compare what he says with what the Bible says. "The Bereans were of more noble character than the Thessalonians, for they received the message with great eagerness and examined the

Scriptures every day to see if what Paul said was true" (Acts 17:11). A preacher who is honestly trying to preach the truth will appreciate the people who have their Bibles open and study with him, because the source of truth is the Scripture, not the minister.

You help the minister stay true by squaring his preaching with the Bible. One Sunday, when preaching on Abraham, I said that Genesis 22:2 was the first time that love was mentioned in the Bible. I got a note from a 16-year-old girl studying Genesis in Bible Bowl. It read, "Genesis 20:13 is the first time 'love' is used. This is what it says: 'This is how you can show your love to me: Everywhere we go, say of me, 'He is my brother.'" Isn't that great? She searched the Scriptures. What an alert, smart-aleck girl! The word *love* is not used in the King James, it's used in the *New International Version.*

A minister can be right on target in one area of his life and way off in another. A minister can be true to the gospel at one period of his life and then change his stance years later. Keep examining the Scripture to see if what he says is true. The people who followed Jim Jones didn't.

Be *prayerful.* "Prayerless pews make powerless pulpits." Make a covenant to pray for one of the ministers of your church every day. Every day. Pray that we'll remain faithful in our personal life. Pray that we'll seek God's will. Pray that we'll have wisdom and energy in leading. James said, "the prayer of a righteous man is powerful and effective" (James 5:16).

Be *encouraging.* People treat me really well. I don't know of a preacher in the country who has a greater blessing than I do. But it's important to be kind and loving toward the other staff people as well. Some of them don't get as many ego boosts as the senior minister does. Some of them get more criticism than I do. They need assistance and they need your encouragement. Show respect for their position.

Recently on a retreat, I asked the church staff to list some of the ways people could encourage them. Here are a few things they said.

1. Get excited about new ideas and be willing to try new methods with them. Show your enthusiasm. Volunteer to help in needed areas without being asked. When we were planning our church picnic, a number of people came up to our Activities Director and said, "I know you have this picnic coming up, is there some way I can help?" You don't even have to be a member. Just say, "I know there's something going on, I think I can help out. What can I do?"

2. Then be responsible. If you've volunteered to help out, follow through without having to be badgered.

3. Occasionally send a note or make a phone call and just let them know that they're appreciated. We all need that.

4. Be realistic in your expectations of their personal life. They're not perfect.

5. Love them enough to confront them personally. If their children are misbehaving, don't talk to other people about it, talk to them.

6. Have a reasonable respect for their home life. If you need them for some reason, if it can wait until the next day, why not wait and contact them at the office? Or look up a telephone number yourself instead of calling their home and asking them to look it up for you.

7. Encourage their spouses, too The unsung heroes of the church are the mates who often are the last ones to leave the church and who have to be onstage a lot. One of the nicest things that you can do for me is to encourage my mate, and every staff member would say the same about his or her spouse.

There's a story in Exodus 17 about the day that Israel battled the army of Amalekites. Moses, the leader of God's people, didn't go into the battle. Instead he stood at the top of the hill and held out the staff of God. "As long as Moses held up his hands, the Israelites were winning, but whenever he lowered his hands, the Amalekites were winning. When Moses' hands grew tired, they took a stone and put it under him, and he sat on it. Aaron and Hur held his hands up—one on one side, one on the other—so that his hands remained steady till sunset. So Joshua overcame the Amalekite army with the sword" (Exodus 17:11-13).

That's still the task of God's people. There's an awesome spiritual battle going on, and the ministers are to be God's leaders in the battle. As they go, so goes the church. When our arms grow weary and our spirits grow weak, it is the congregation's task to undergird and support until the victory is won.

# Be Good Citizens

## Titus 3:1, 2

SAMUEL JOHNSON SAID, "We don't need to be taught new ideas so much as we need to be reminded of old truths." Paul begins the third chapter by telling Titus to "remind the people to be the kind of citizens of their country they should be." We know we live in a wonderful country, but we have a tendency to forget that and take it for granted. We know we're supposed to be model citizens of that country, but we need to be reminded how. We know that as members of the church, we ought to be the backbone of our nation, but we need to be reminded of that regularly.

This section of Titus 3 suggests three practical ways that we Christians can make a positive contribution to our country. It reminds us that if we're going to represent the Lord well, the individual members of the church ought to be outstanding citizens. These suggestions are not dramatic, but they constitute the heart and soul of what makes America special.

### Be Respectful of Governmental Authority

"Remind the people to be subject to rulers and authorities" (v. 1). Romans 13 is a parallel passage that gives us details about how to be obedient to the government. Paul writes, "Everyone must submit himself to the governing authorities, for there is no authority except that which God has established. The authorities that exist have been established by God" (Romans 13:1). This doesn't mean that God put Hitler or Idi Amin in office. It means that government is one of three spheres of authority that God has established: the home, the church, and the government. He established those authorities so that there would be order in the world He created.

"Consequently, he who rebels against the authority is rebelling against what God has instituted, and those who do so will bring judgment on themselves. For rulers hold no terror for those who do right, but for those who do wrong. Do you want to be free from fear of the one in authority? Then do what is right and he will commend you. For he is God's servant to do you good. But if you do wrong, be afraid, for he does not bear the sword for nothing" (Romans 13:2-4a).

Be afraid if you do wrong. You know what it's like when you're driving your car on the interstate with the cruise control set at 65, and suddenly you come across a hidden police radar unit. You don't mind because you're obeying the law. You just go on. But if you're cruising at 75 or 80, and you suddenly go by one of those hidden police radar units, your heart starts pounding, your hands tremble, and you look in the rear view mirror to see if he's coming after you—because you're afraid. (At least, that's what I'm *told* people feel.)

Paul goes on to say, "He is God's servant, an agent of wrath to bring punishment on the wrongdoer. Therefore, it is necessary to submit to the authorities, not only because of possible punishment but also because of conscience" (Romans 13:4b, 5).

A preacher who had been guilty of shoplifting said he had a difficult time preaching because of a guilty conscience. One Sunday morning, a policeman in their church got up to open a window. "When that policeman got up and started walking down the side aisle, I thought he was going to come and arrest me right in public," he said. "I could barely keep preaching because of a guilty conscience."

Paul goes on to say, "This is also why you pay taxes, for the authorities are God's servants, who give their full time to governing. Give everyone what you owe him: If you owe taxes, pay taxes; if revenue, then revenue; if respect, then respect; if honor, then honor" (Romans 13:6, 7). Jesus lived under an oppressive dictatorship, but Jesus said, "Give to Caesar what is Caesar's, and to God what is God's" (Matthew 22:21). This means several practical things for us. First, it means we should respect government authorities even if they are imperfect. Since these institutions are all headed up by people, they are all imperfect. But their source of authority is God, and we are to honor the position. I will never forget Dan Rather, CBS newscaster, attempting to humiliate President Nixon during a press conference. Nixon had done some things wrong, but I thought that Rather stepped over the line in not respecting his position enough.

Contrast that with David in the Old Testament. When King Saul was trying to kill David, Saul was abusing his authority. Saul was a madman, evidently a manic depressive. David was hiding with his men in the deep recesses of a cave when King Saul, not knowing he was there, came to the mouth of the cave to rest. David's men whispered to him, "the Lord has delivered your adversary into your hand. Take his life and the throne will be yours." David tiptoed up to the sleeping king and took his sword and cut off a little piece of Saul's robe. But David didn't take his life. When he went back to his men, they urged him to kill Saul, but David felt guilty even about cutting his robe: "The Lord forbid that I should do such a thing to my master, the Lord's anointed, or lift my hand against him; for he is the anointed of the Lord" (1 Samuel 24:6). With these words, David rebuked his men and did not allow them to attack Saul. Saul left the cave and went on his way.

We're to be respectful of government officials for their

position, even if their character is not perfect. We need to be careful about the Dan Quayle jokes, for example, that they don't get too disrespectful. Although you may not agree with those in leadership positions, don't humiliate them or ridicule them. When you have your children in the presence of the mayor, or the congressman, or the county judge, teach them to show respect. You don't have to cower in their presence or act like a puppy dog around them, but respect their position.

We are also to be obedient to the law, even if it's unreasonable. "Be subject to rulers and authorities," and "be obedient" (v. 1). It's easier to obey a law when you agree with it than when you disagree with it, and there are a lot of inconsistencies in America. Some wit asks, "Where else but in America do they lock up the jury and let the prisoner go free? Where else but in America does it take more brains to fill out your income tax than it does to make the money originally? Where else but in America does a mother drive her kids three blocks to a physical fitness center?" There are a lot of inconsistencies in our country. Some laws don't make sense, either, and it's difficult to obey them, but we are to be subject and obedient.

I recently stopped at a red light at an uncongested intersection. The sign said, "No Turn on Red." I thought, "What a stupid place to have a No Turn on Red sign." There was no traffic coming, no pedestrians, and no policeman in sight. But I sat there and waited for 35-40 seconds for that light to change, just so I could use it in a sermon illustration about being obedient. But even if nobody sees you, and even if you're not going to use it for a sermon illustration, be obedient to the law even if you disagree.

The only time we have the right to disobey the law is when it forces us to disobey God's commandments. If there is a man-made law that is in direct conflict with God's instructions in the Bible, we are to disobey. Acts 4 says that Peter and John were told not to preach in the name of Jesus. They said, "We've got to obey Jesus, not man." Besides government officials and laws, we should also respect the symbols of our country, even if they just represent the government.

Symbols were important in the Bible. God placed a rainbow in the sky as a symbol that he would never destroy the world with a flood again. God gave us Communion as a symbol of the death of Jesus. Baptism is a symbol of the burial and resurrection of Christ. For 200 years, our country has had symbols that provide an opportunity for Christians to remember and show respect for their country.

The Supreme Court has ruled that it is not a violation of the Constitution to burn the American flag. *Time* magazine had an excellent subtitle to its story on that subject. It read, "The Right to Burn the Flag, a Good Reason Not To." If we live in a nation that values freedom so much that you're free even to abuse its flag, we ought to respect the freedom that flag symbolizes enough not to do it. People in China and eastern Europe have died for what that flag symbolizes. Christians ought to respect the flag. We ought to be able to repeat the Pledge of Allegiance with feeling. It is not worshiping the state to show respect. Years ago, people worshiped their country, but now the pendulum has gone to the opposite extreme. It's not worshiping the country to show respect; it's worshiping the God who is the giver of every good and perfect gift.

We ought to respect the national anthem when it's played. One of my pet peeves is to see people talking or walking around, paying no attention when the national anthem is played before a ball game. Some people don't even bother to stand up. The least we can do is to teach our children to stand quietly or sing enthusiastically during the national anthem. It reminds us what a privileged people we are.

We also have a responsibility to serve in public office, even if it may be frustrating. We do not live under a dictatorship, but a democracy, and we have the opportunity of serving in positions of authority. God appointed David, Joseph, Daniel, and other Bible people to lead the nation. He still calls some Christian people to do that today. If God leads you to serve in public office, you heed that call, even though it is a thankless and often frustrating job. I've never talked to a Christian politician who didn't express frustration that they couldn't make more of a difference. Edward Hale said, "I'm only one man, but I am one. I can't do everything, but I can do something. What I can do, I ought to do, and what I ought to do by the grace of God, I will do."

## Be Diligent in Your Occupation

"Be ready for any honest work," paraphrases *The Living Bible*. The King James Version says, "Be ready to do every good work." The following notice was posted in a Chicago store in 1858, "This store will be open from 6:00 a.m. to 9:00 p.m. the year round. On arrival each morning, the store must be swept; counters, shelves, and showcases dusted. Lamps must be trimmed, pens made, a pail of water and bucket of coal brought in before breakfast. After 14 hours of work, leisure hours should be spent in reading."

A hundred years ago, people worked hard. This nation was carved out of the wilderness by people's bare hands. I saw the Oregon Trail recently, and I could hardly believe what the pioneers endured. They took their families in covered wagons and climbed over the Rocky Mountains braving the elements, disease, and attacks by Indians. They were made of a different stock than we are. Now, social scientists are talking about a workless society. R. F. Norton, in his article, "The New Leisure," says, "Some social scientists foresee the time, perhaps in the next 25 or even 10 years, when people constituting 2% of our population can do the necessary work to provide food and consumer goods for the remaining 98%. Then state governments will establish Departments of Leisure to balance Departments of Labor."

The Walt Disney Corporation is now spending $16 billion to expand Disney World. When we have people living in tar paper shacks, when we have illegal immigrants picking fruit for pennies, when one out of four young people do not graduate from high school in our state, doesn't it seem inconsistent that we're spending $16 billion to play? In a world where the Japanese have already outpaced American productivity; where in the year 1992, it's predicted that a united Europe will push American productivity to third-ranking in the world, don't you wonder if we can afford $16 billion for entertainment in one spot?

In the fifth century B.C., when Athens was at its peak, it was said that when the people of Athens sought freedom from responsibility, Athens would no longer be free. A nation that is soft and lazy is ripe for a fall. It doesn't have to be a military takeover, it can be an economic takeover, or just an erosion of values. One historian said, "The history of civilizations is really just the patter of silken slippers descending the stairs, and the thunder of hobnailed boots coming up."

We can strengthen our country and make it more stable by working hard. "Make it your ambition to lead a quiet life, to mind your own business and to work with your hands just as we told you, so that your daily life may win the respect of outsiders and so that you will not be dependent on anybody" (1 Thessalonians 4:11, 12). We cannot be a strong nation if nobody is working. We're not going to get rich standing around in a circle with our hands in each other's pockets. One of the best things we can do for our country is to work to support our families and pay our taxes so that those who are needy will be able to survive. It's also a good testimony to outsiders when our faith makes a difference in the workplace.

Larry Burkett is a nationally-known Christian lecturer and writer who conducts seminars on how to manage your money. He received a letter from a non-Christian woman who owned a small business. She wrote, "I've had trouble with my employees for years. They will not do an honest day's work. They are lazy and rebellious. I heard your radio program and decided to hire all Christians. I did, but I have never had a more complaining, griping group of people. They were always mumbling about something. I've now replaced them with refugees. The refugees are so grateful to work, they'll do everything I ask. They don't grumble and complain. I think American Christians need to wake up." Maybe she just had a chip on her shoulder, or maybe her experience will change with the passing of time. But the truth is, we Christian people can be just as lazy and complaining as the world around us.

Proverbs 6 says, "Go to the ant, you sluggard; consider its ways and be wise! It has no commander, no overseer or ruler, yet it stores its provisions in summer and gathers its food at harvest. How long will you lie there, you sluggard?" The meaning of America is not to be found in life without toil. Freedom is not only bought with a great price, it is maintained by diligence.

## Be Considerate of Others

"Slander no one, . . . be peaceable and considerate, and show true humility toward all men" (v. 2). When Alexis De Touqueville, the European historian, visited America years ago, he said, "America is great because America is good. When America ceases to be good, it won't be great anymore." There's a significant element in our society who are not good. They make no pretense at being selfless. They will lie, deceive, maim, or kill in order to get their way. And it's not just the addict from the ghetto who has that mentality. Many prominent people care about nobody but themselves. Some managers actually get bonuses for cutting employee benefits and for being as ruthless as they can be.

But Jesus said, "Do unto others as you would have them do unto you." The best thing that we can do for our country is to treat other people right. That's not dramatic, it doesn't make headlines, but if half the people in this country who called themselves Christian would practice the Golden Rule, our nation could be strong and great again.

Alice Roosevelt, the daughter of Teddy Roosevelt, was known for having a caustic tongue. Her slogan was, "If you can't say anything good about somebody, come sit by me." Some Christians are like that: "Tell me all the gossip and slander so I can pass it on." Their favorite song is, "I Love to

Tell the Story." Paul said in Titus 1:12 that the Cretans were liars, but the Christians on the island were to be different. He said, "Don't slander anybody." They were to be distinctive and practice the very un-Cretan activity of telling the truth and being kind to people.

"Be peaceable," Paul writes. Don't be always spoiling for a fight. Don't look for a quarrel. Don't be threatening to sue your neighbor every time you get a chance.

One of my favorite comic strips is the Wizard of Id. One day Rodney, one of the warriors, came in from a battle. His helmet was teetering. He was bruised and battered, and his horse was crippled, listing to one side.

The king said, "Where've you been?"

"Out fighting your enemies on the west," he said. "I've pillaged, and I've burned, and I've killed your enemies on the west."

"I don't have any enemies on the west," the king said.

"You do now," Rodney said.

Don't go out of your way to make enemies. "If it is possible, as far as it depends on you, live at peace with everyone" (Romans 12:18). It's not always possible. There will always be some people you can't live peaceably with. But don't be the source of conflict. Make every effort to live in harmony with those around you. Don't stir up trouble.

"Be considerate," he writes. Think about the other person's feelings ahead of your own. If there is one thing wrong with this country today, it's that everybody feels obligated to stand up for his rights. The ACLU stands up for rights and freedom, but the Christian is to look for opportunities to be submissive and to be a servant of others. What a difference! The Greek word here for *be considerate* means, "does not stand on the letter of the law; considers the intent of the other as well as the action." The King James translates it as "gentle."

Paul concludes by saying, "Show true humility toward all men" (v. 2). Humility. Tom Nichol tells a story about Bobby Knight, coach of Indiana's basketball team. When Knight was in Louisiana, he saw a bolt of red cloth that he thought would make a great IU jacket. He bought the cloth, took it to his tailor in Bloomington, and asked him to make a jacket. The tailor said, "There's not enough cloth here for me to make a jacket for you."

Bobby Knight was disappointed, but he held onto the cloth. Weeks later, he was in Lexington, Kentucky and saw a tailor there. "Could you make me a jacket out of this cloth?" he asked.

The tailor in Lexington said, "Sure. I can make you a jacket, a pair of trousers, and a vest out of that cloth."

Bobby Knight said, "My tailor in Indiana told me there wasn't enough cloth here even to make a jacket. How can you do all that?"

You've got to understand," he said, "you're just not as big down here in Kentucky as you are up there in Indiana."

You may be big in certain circles, but show true humility towards all men. The *Revised Standard Version* translates this, "Show perfect courtesy towards all men." Don't bully people. Don't strut like you're superior. Treat people with courtesy. Note that important phrase, "toward all men." Be courteous not just towards those who can reciprocate or those who are on the same socioeconomic level as you. Toward all men. That means you treat the waitress with the same kindness that you do the owner of the restaurant. That means that you're as polite to the cab driver as you are the airplane pilot. That means you're as kind to the janitor as you are the principal. Be courteous to all men. Do unto others as you would have them do unto you.

Deep down, we're not convinced that practicing the Golden Rule and being considerate of other people is going to make much of a difference in our nation. We think we're too far gone for that. What we need is force. What we need is political power. What we need are lobbying efforts. What we need are the right people in office. There's a constant temptation, even for the Christian, to put his confidence in the love of power, rather than the power of love.

Sociologist Tony Campolo said, "I remember when Martin Luther King came marching out of Selma and met old Bull

Connor. Bull Connor had guns, clubs and troops. King and his followers got down on their knees and prayed. Then at the count of ten, Connor and his troops charged in." Campolo said, "I watched on live television as King and the others got battered, beaten, and plastered all over that road. And when Martin Luther King and his followers did not retaliate, I knew that they had won. Oh, it looked like they were defeated, but love was stronger than power."

Campolo wrote, "The biblical Jesus wants a church that changes the world not from a position of power, but from a position of love and commitment. Christians who follow the cultural Jesus seem to have the idea that if we get enough power, if we can get enough people into office, if we can just take over America, we can force America to be righteous. Why didn't Jesus think of that?" He added, "I believe that we have to change the world with the weapons of the church, rather than with the weapons of the world. We have another style, another way. It's loving servanthood. It's giving ourselves. It's moving in and caring; it's loving; it's redeeming and not destroying."

We are privileged to live in the greatest country the world has ever seen. Everyone would concur that there has been an erosion of principle over the last several years. But it's now more critical than ever that the people who belong to the church of Jesus Christ make their influence known. Not just political power, or economic power, not even just voting power, but most importantly, the power of Jesus Christ who loved us and gave himself up for us. That means we respect authority as long as it doesn't violate God's Word. It means we work diligently even though many around us are slothful. It means that we treat all people with love, even though hate seems to dominate. And it means most of all, that we trust in the Lord Jesus Christ who will one day return as King of all countries and Lord of all governments.

George Washington wrote this prayer centuries ago:

Almighty God, we make our earnest prayer that thou will keep the United States in thy holy protection. That thou wilt incline the heads of the citizens to cultivate a spirit of subordination and obedience to government, and entertain a brotherly affection and love for one another and for their fellow citizens of the United States at large. And finally, that thou wilt most graciously be pleased to dispose us all to do justice, to love mercy, and to demean ourselves with that charity, humility and pacific temper of mind which were the characteristics of the divine author of our blessed religion, and with a humble imitation of whose example in these things we can ever hope to be a happy nation. Grant our supplication, we beseech thee. Through Jesus Christ, our Lord, Amen.

# Develop a Sweet Spirit

## Titus 3:3-8

OVER TWENTY YEARS ago I read, in a book by Bruce Larson, a chapter title that I've never forgotten: "Are You Fun to Live With?" The more we grow to be like Jesus Christ, the chapter said, the easier it ought to be for other people to be around us.

Jesus Christ himself was an enjoyable person to be around. He once said, "Take my yoke upon you and learn from me, for I am gentle and humble in heart, and you will find rest for your souls. For my yoke is easy and my burden is light" (Matthew 11:29, 30). Jesus did not make life miserable for those around Him. On the contrary, His followers found His companionship made their lives better. It was easy to be with Him.

All kinds of people were attracted to Jesus Christ. Sinners like the woman at the well, intellectuals like Nicodemus, and doubters like Thomas. All kinds of people were comfortable in the presence of Christ. He said, "If I be lifted up, I will draw all men to me." His closest friends loved being around Him. When He died, not one of His disciples said, "Well that's a relief, Jesus was so insensitive and demanding that I'm glad He's gone. I felt ill-at-ease in His presence." On the contrary, they mourned His passing. They missed His fellowship. They were overjoyed when He arose from the dead and they could be with Him again.

In His final words to them, Jesus said, "Peace I leave with you; my peace I give you," and "As I have loved you, so must you love one another" (John 14:27; 13:34).

Jesus had a congenial spirit about Him that attracted people. The more we grow to be like Christ, the more His disposition should be reflected in us. Christians should not be mean-spirited, quick-tempered, hypercritical people. We ought to be developing inside us a pleasantness that makes us easy to live with. One of the most valuable qualities in a marriage partner is a sweet spirit. Solomon had been married a number of times—700, to be exact. Solomon said, "Better to live in a desert than with a quarrelsome and ill-tempered wife" (Proverbs 21:19). It's a joy to live with someone who is pleasant, but it's miserable to live with somebody who has a sour disposition, no matter how physically attractive he or she may be.

That's true in the church, too. If the church is going to represent Jesus Christ, there ought to be a sweet spirit in the church. Eleanor Daniel, a Christian author and professor, visited our church a number of years ago. "If I could describe Southeast Christian Church in a word," she said, "it would be the word 'joy.' People seemed to be glad to be there. A spirit of joy seemed to permeate the church." I've been to churches that could be described in a negative word, haven't you? Contentious, legalistic, tense, weak, disbelieving, sour, worldly, dead. But the Lord wants His church to have a sweet disposition.

The Bible says of the early church that there was gladness and singleness of heart. David said, "I rejoiced with those who said to me, 'Let us go to the house of the Lord.'" I like the chorus, "There's a sweet, sweet spirit in this place, and I know it's the Spirit of the Lord."

Titus 3:3-8 instructs us to get rid of malice, envy, and hatred, and to devote ourselves to kindness and doing what is good. Most importantly, it talks about the reason we ought to be sweet-spirited. If we're not pleasant in spirit, it's because we've forgotten what God has done for us or we haven't really allowed Him to transform us. Once we understand who we are in Jesus Christ, we can't help but to have a new disposition.

## What We Once Were

Paul begins by reminding us what we once were without Christ. There's a sense of orientation here. Verse 3 tells us in relationship to God we were once foolish. The Bible says that a *fool* is somebody who says in his heart that there is no God. A man doesn't have to be an atheist to be a fool, he's just one who doesn't honor God. He does not acknowledge God's authority over his life. A man can be brilliant, wealthy, and have several diplomas, but if he does not honor God, and God's Word, he is a fool. The Bible says, "What good will it be for a man if he gains the whole world, yet forfeits his soul?" (Matthew 16:26) That's being foolish.

We were disobedient to God. In our pride, were determined to prove that we were self-sufficient. We defied God's instructions about putting others ahead of ourselves, being generous with our money, and abiding by His moral values. In the words of Frank Sinatra's song, "We did it our way."

We were deceived. If a man is wrong about God, and he's wrong about God's Word, then he's vulnerable to all kinds of false philosophies. He's vulnerable to fantasies. "There is a way that seems right to a man, but in the end it leads to death" (Proverbs 14:12). The enemy of our souls is feeding us with all kinds of deceiving philosophy that will destroy us in the end. "You want to be excited and happy, then have an affair," he whispers. "Go ahead and get yourself into debt for things you don't need. That will make you prosperous." "Go ahead and take drugs and alcohol. That will calm you down." "Go ahead and step on everybody to get to the top. That will make you successful." But in the end, we are miserable and unhappy.

Hugh Hefner, the promoter of the "playboy philosophy," finally got married. The one who ridiculed marriage, who made fun of the principle one man for one woman, now, in his latter years, wants the security of a commitment and marries a woman 35 years younger than he. What a testimony to the futility of a life without God. How inconsistent! The media seemed oblivious to the inconsistency of it all, and they just played it up as another phase of Hefner's life. The world just goes on being deceived and deceiving others.

Paul says that in relationship to God, "we were foolish, disobedient, deceived," but in relationship to ourselves, we were "enslaved by all types of passions and pleasures" (v. 3). A person starts out to sin and it's fun for a little while. But, eventually, the fun wears off, and we become enslaved to it. A law of increased appetite and diminishing return takes over. We talk about a person being entangled in an affair, consumed by greed, or addicted to drugs, alcohol, or pornography.

"Don't you know that when you offer yourself to someone to obey him as slaves, you are slaves to the one whom you obey—whether you are slaves to sin, which leads to death, or to obedience, which leads to righteousness?" (Romans 6:16) Stuart Briscoe wrote, "If pleasure is the watchword of our lives, we can only be happy when we're having a pleasurable experience. Then we must never be bored and never engage in anything mundane or routine." He adds, "We spend all our time, money, and energy trying to avoid the real world and we become enslaved by the desire to escape reality."

In relationship to other people, we were full of malice (seething anger looking to get even) and envy (resentment of what another person has and delight at his misfortune). We were "being hated and hating one another" (v. 3b). When you hate somebody, they usually retaliate. It's a vicious cycle. You hate them, they hate you.

Heavyweight boxing champion Mike Tyson was a subject of a derogatory book by a former friend, Jose Torrez. In the book, Tyson was disclosed as "throwing his best punches at the women he loves." Tyson was later interviewed on television. He was bitter and he vowed to get even. That's the way it is in the world. If you're hateful, you're hated in return. The person without God isn't much fun to live with. There are occasional moments of pleasure, but in rebelling against God, we become bitter against one another.

Paul says, "At one time, we too were . . . disobedient" (v. 3). He's not talking about other people. He himself was like that. He was a fool. He rejected Jesus Christ, and he was breathing out threats and slaughter against the church. Saul of Tarsus was selfishly ambitious and not much fun to be around until the Lord Jesus Christ got hold of his life.

## What God Did

He goes on to say, let's remember what God did for us. "When the kindness and love of God our Savior appeared, he saved us, not because of righteous things we had done, but because of his mercy" (v. 4, 5). God showed kindness to us when we had been unkind to Him. If God had responded in a human way, He would have retaliated. He would have said, "I am the creator of your souls. I'm the one who made you. Rebel against Me and I'm going to wipe you off the map." But instead, He broke the cycle of hatred and responded in mercy and kindness. Just at the right time, when we were still powerless, Christ died for the ungodly.

Donald Barnhouse told of a fire that swept over his dad's farm, a prairie fire. Afterward, when his dad was walking across the farm, he kicked a lump of charcoal that he thought was a stump. When he did, little baby chicks ran out from beneath it. Closer examination revealed that it wasn't just a burned stump. The lump was the remains of a mother hen who had seen that her little chicks would not be able to escape the sweeping flames. She gathered them under her wings and sat there and endured the fire herself that her chicks might live.

That was Christ's response to us. Knowing that we would be engulfed and destroyed by the sin that so easily besets us, He voluntarily remained on the cross to absorb all the fiery blows of the evil one that we might live.

Paul says that through Jesus' death on the cross, there are three benefits. He lists them here.

First, we are saved. He saved us. You hear a lot of talk in Christian circles about being saved. What does it mean? When we're saved from something, it's usually some danger—from an embarrassing moment, from financial disaster, from drowning. The Bible says Christians are saved. We're saved from the wrath of God. We're saved from the ominous consequences of our sin.

Another benefit is that He poured out His Holy Spirit on us generously, through Jesus Christ, our Lord. When we become Christians, God cleanses our hearts of sin and fills our hearts with the indwelling of the Holy Spirit. The Holy Spirit then gives us increasing power in the Christian life. Power to overcome temptation. Power to testify about our faith. Power to understand Scripture. Power to witness to other people; to love the unlovely.

I hear people say, "I haven't become a Christian yet, but I'm not sure I can live the life and I don't want to be a hypocrite." If you wait to get your life straightened out, you'll never respond to Christ, because being a Christian is saying, "Lord, I am sinful. I need You to cleanse me. I am weak, I need you to empower me through Your Holy Spirit." In the first gospel sermon ever preached, Peter said to the people in Jerusalem, "You have crucified the Son of God."

The people believed it. "What shall we do?" they asked.

Peter responded, "Repent and be baptized, every one of you, in the name of Jesus Christ so that your sins may be forgiven. And you will receive the gift of the Holy Spirit" (Acts 2:38).

The third benefit that Christ gives us is the promise of eternal life. "So that, having been justified by his grace, we might become heirs having the hope of eternal life" (v. 7). He promises that when we accept Him, we will live with Him forever in Heaven after we die. That's not just wishful thinking. It's not just something we say at a funeral. That's a fact based on Jesus Christ who died and rose from the grave.

He said, "Because I live, you can live, too. Even though you die, yet shall you live again" (John 11:25, 26).

Think for a minute how incredibly kind God has been to us. We were foolish and rebellious, but instead of punishing us, He came to us and He saved us through the death of Jesus Christ on the cross. He gives us the Holy Spirit to empower us, and He promises that He's going to take us to be with Him in Heaven when we die. "Grace is absurd to the human mind," Max Lucado said. "In fact, the only thing more absurd than the gift is our stubborn unwillingness to receive it."

## What We Are to Become

Since we have been saved by Christ, we are to become like Him. Our life is to be changed. "If anyone is in Christ, he is a new creature; the old has gone, the new has come!" (2 Corinthians 5:17)

Our doctrinal beliefs change. We once were fools who rejected God, now we believe in Him. Our moral values change. We were once disobedient, now we seek to walk by His moral standards. Our attitudes and personalities change, too. We were once envious, filled with bitterness and wrath; now, the love, peace, and joy of Jesus Christ are to be part of our disposition. "Your attitude should be the same as that of Jesus Christ" (Philippians 2:5).

On the Fourth of July, I put some hamburgers on the grill and then it started to rain. I had to stand in the garage and run out to turn the hamburgers over, and I got pretty wet. Then it stopped raining and I took my boys golfing. I walked with them eighteen holes, carrying my bag. It was hot, and I perspired a lot. I just wanted to show them that I could do it and still beat them, which I did. I came home exhausted and sweaty, and laid down on the couch and took a nap. I woke up about suppertime. My wife came in and said, "Boy, it smells like a locker room in here." She was followed by my teenage son, who said, "Dad, you stink!" I can take a hint, so right before supper I took a shower. And after I showered, I didn't put on those same sweaty, smelly clothes and come back to supper! I put on clean clothes. Once you're cleansed, you want to put on clean, fresh clothes. Everyone else wants you to change too!

When we become Christians, Jesus washes us clean of any odorous thing we have ever done. Peter speaks of the washing of rebirth. "Baptism . . . now saves you also—not the removal of dirt from the body but the pledge of a good conscience toward God. It saves you by the resurrection of Jesus Christ" (1 Peter 3:21). When we accept Jesus Christ as Savior, we confess Him. We're baptized into Him. The blood of Christ cleanses us of our sin and we are washed clean. To go back to our former moral values, beliefs, and attitudes is like putting on the filthy garments of the past that don't belong. "A sow that is washed goes back to her wallowing in the mud" (2 Peter 2:22). Some Christians change in moral values and change in beliefs, but somehow never transform their attitude.

Recently I stood outside between services just to watch what goes on in our church parking lot. An elderly woman was driving in, and she must have forgotten something, because she decided she wanted to go back out. Rather than going all the way around the parking lot with the flow of traffic, she started to do a U-turn, which meant she had to go across three lanes of traffic. Everybody was supposed to stop for her. When she started turning, the fellow directing traffic started yelling, "No Ma'am, no Ma'am, you need to go on, go all the way around." She just kept turning, inching around. He jumped in front of the car and said, "Ma'am, you'll have to turn and go all the way around the lot." She just kept inching right at him, and he kept backing up. Finally, he had to jump aside and wave her on through. (I didn't recognize her. I think she must have been visiting from somewhere outside of town. None of our people have that kind of spirit!)

"Your attitude should be the same as that of Christ Jesus," who "made himself nothing, taking the very nature of a servant," (Philippians 2:5, 7). When we're proud, stubborn, and arrogant, when we demand our own way all the time, we've got all those old smelly garments still on. The Bible says, "And the peace of God, which transcends all understanding, will guard your hearts and your minds in Christ Jesus" (Philippians 4:7).

Our attitude and disposition can make all the difference in the world. Back in 1981 the North American Christian Convention was in Louisville, and its theme was, "In All Things Love." Our church was in charge of registrations then. On the first night, a preacher came up to the registration booth and said, "I don't like this badge you gave me. It's not as nice as the ones you gave out earlier and I'd like another one."

The woman said, "I'm sorry, but we're out of those. We can retype that one."

"No!" he said. "I don't want one like this. I want one like you had before!"

"Sir, you don't understand," the woman said. "A number of preachers came in with last-minute registrations that we didn't plan on. We ran out of that style."

"Well, I'm a preacher, and I brought mine in at the last minute, and that doesn't make any difference," he said. "I want one of those that says, 'In All Things Love' on it, do you understand?"

We didn't understand.

Here was a guy who knew the Bible, but somehow, he never built the bridge between what the Scripture (and the theme of the convention) says and his own personal attitude. I see that all the time. "To this you were called, because Christ suffered for you, leaving you an example, that you should follow in his steps. He committed no sin, and no deceit was found in his mouth. When they hurled their insults at him, he did not retaliate; when he suffered, he made no threats. Instead, he entrusted himself to the one who judges justly" (1 Peter 2:21-3). Christ gave you an example, so you should follow in His steps in attitude, too.

Look back over these six verses in Titus 3 and circle the characteristics of God that we should emulate. These attitudes make a sweet-spirited church. Verse 3 talks about

God's kindness. The church should be a place where people are kind to one another. They are courteous in the parking lot. They smile and help each other in the vestibule. They offer help to newcomers with children who don't know where to go. They are kind to elderly and infirm people. There is no place in the spirit of the church for a defiant or "me first" spirit. The fruit of the spirit is kindness. Robert Schuller said, "It would be amazing at how much we could influence for Christ if we would just treat people nice."

Verse 3 also speaks of God's love. The world is full of hatred, but the church should be full of compassion. Love is kind. Love does not envy. Love does not demand its own way. Love does not keep a record of wrong. Love protects. Love never fails (1 Corinthians 13).

Paul Harvey and his wife were visiting a church in which the minister was talking about the importance of touching to communicate love. To illustrate his point, the minister said, "It's a proven fact that a newborn baby gains weight 50% faster if the baby is touched and coddled."

Paul Harvey said his wife leaned over and said to him, "Don't you dare touch me."

But the church should be a place where we gain spiritual strength and spiritual pounds because we're not ashamed to show love.

Verse 5 speaks of God's mercy. The church should stand for the truth, but it should also be merciful toward sinners or people who make mistakes. Don't have a judgmental spirit. Don't always be looking for something wrong. One preacher said he deliberately put a mistake in the bulletin every week, so that the people who loved to find a mistake would be happy when they went home. Don't demand that others be perfect. Be merciful. Jesus said, "Blessed are the merciful, for they will receive mercy" (Matthew 5:7).

Verse 6 speaks of God's generosity. He poured out the Holy Spirit on us generously. A sweet-spirited church is a generous church. It is not more concerned about nickels and dimes than it is about people. Christian people within the church should be models of benevolence. Recently, I mentioned a couple in our church who had experienced extreme illness and a long hospital stay. Their insurance hadn't covered all their expenses and they were in financial stress. Before three days passed, several anonymous donors had given $6,000 to help cover their costs. That's generosity. But it doesn't have to be big things. It's in your attitude towards the little things.

Parents attending the North American Christian Convention were invited to bring their elementary-age child at 9:00 in the morning, and that child would receive care all day long until 5:00 in the afternoon. The children's workers would not only provide good supervision, but a meal for that child at noon, and they would also take the child on a bus trip to Santa Claus Land, Indiana or to the zoo. All this for a cost of $10.00. Volunteer workers were astonished that people called in complaining about the cost! "I have two children. They're charging me $20.00 for my kids. There ought to be some kind of alternative. That seems like a lot of money for somebody coming to worship the Lord!" But other people called in, saying, "I can't believe how much we're getting for just $10.00. Incredible!" The difference was not between who had money and those who didn't. The difference was that of attitude and disposition.

Verse 7 speaks of God's grace; "having been justified by his grace." Mercy forgives faults and grace expresses goodness to those who deserve punishment. A sweet-spirited church is anxious to forgive, restore, and bless. A sweet-spirited church doesn't hold it against people forever if they make a mistake. We don't say, "I remember 15 years ago they got a divorce," or "I remember before she got married, she was pregnant," or "I remember him using some bad language years ago." We know how to forgive and to restore. We extend the same latitude towards others that we want God to extend to us.

One Sunday just after church, I was heading home and saw a three-car accident ahead of me. It was just a fender-bender, in which people banged into the rear end of each other. The police were there, and people were standing around. When I got close, I saw that all three people involved in the accident were from our church, and the policeman was from our church, too. I rolled the window down. Somebody smiled and said, "Go ahead, preacher. We've got it all under control." They weren't standing around holding hands singing, "Sweet, Sweet Spirit in This Place," but there was still a pleasant disposition in spite of adversity.

"I want you to stress these things, so that those who have trusted in God may be careful to devote themselves to doing what is good" (v. 8). You have to stress these things because it doesn't come easy; you have to work at it. Being sweet-spirited is not the natural reaction after our car is damaged. We have to devote ourselves; we have to be careful. That means we swallow our pride, restrain our tempers, and make the effort to react the way Jesus did. We change our attitude.

A man had been to church one Sunday morning and knew he was supposed to have a changed disposition. He went to catch a bus. He thought he was going to catch it at the last second, but the bus driver, with a sneer on his face, slammed the door, took off, and splashed mud all over the man's suit.

He stood there for a moment, smiled, and said, "May your soul rest in peace . . . and may it be soon."

If we're honest, we'll admit a sweet spirit doesn't come easy. We have to work at it.

"These things are excellent and profitable for everyone" (v. 8). Do you want to be excellent in the Christian life? Change your disposition. Let your attitude be that of Jesus Christ. It will be profitable for you! If you hate people, they will hate you in return. If you're kind to people, they will be kind to you in return. You're reflecting the grace of God. One great preacher used to close every sermon by saying, "God loved you first, now just love Him back."

# Maintain Harmony

## Titus 3:9-15

MY SONS USED to fight a lot. I guess that's normal among children, but it bothered me that they fought and didn't get along. One of my lowest days as a father was when they were both teenagers. I heard them shouting and banging around in a room upstairs, and I bolted up there to break up a nasty fist fight. I know you can't *imagine* such a thing happening in a preacher's home (we do spend most of our time sitting in a circle reading the Bible and having prayer).

I was disappointed in them. Why couldn't they get along? Our heavenly Father feels much the same way about us. It grieves the heart of God when He sees His people bicker and fight. It thrills the Father to see brothers and sisters in the Lord who have a harmonious relationship.

One of the ways we honor God as a church is by maintaining a spirit of unity. That's not just my speculation—that truth is emphasized all the way through the Bible, even back in the Old Testament before the church was established. "How good and pleasant it is when brothers live together in unity!" (Psalm 133:1). Proverbs 6:16 said there were seven things that God hated, and the last one was a man who stirs up dissension among the brothers. Jesus also emphasized the importance of harmony. He said, "All men will know that you are my disciples if you love one another" (John 13:35). His final prayer in the garden of Gethsemane was, "May they be brought to complete unity to let the world know that you sent me" (John 17:23).

The New Testament church began as a united church. "When the day of Pentecost came, they were all together in one place" (Acts 2:1). "All the believers were one in heart and mind" (Acts 4:32). Many of the New Testament letters appeal to the churches to refrain from division and live in harmony. "Let us therefore make every effort to do what leads to peace and to mutual edification" (Romans 14:19). "I appeal to you, brothers, in the name of our Lord Jesus Christ, that all of you agree with one another, so that there may be no divisions among you and that you may be perfectly united in mind and thought" (1 Corinthians 1:10). "Make every effort to keep the unity of the Spirit through the bond of peace" (Ephesians 4:3). It is a serious matter to create discord in the family of God. When churches bicker, it saps our energy, it quenches our spirit, and it negates our testimony.

One of the reasons that Southeast Christian Church has grown to be a large church is that we've never split. There has been a spirit of harmony in our fellowship from the very beginning. When something threatens that union, people have been mature and have risen above it. If you have ever been in a fighting church, you never want to go back to that. One man had been in a church so battered by division that they'd had three different preachers in three years. He said to me, "I noticed the slogan on your church letterhead, 'Speaking the Truth in Love.' We don't have a slogan at our church, but if we had one it would be, 'If You Want to Fight, Go to First Christian.'" That's sad.

Paul concludes his letter to Titus by writing about the importance of maintaining harmony in the church. His final emphasis is on unity, and it's one we need to take to heart if we're going to heed God's counsel to a growing church.

## Avoid Controversy if Possible

"Avoid foolish controversies and genealogies and arguments and quarrels about the law" (v. 9). Avoid *foolish* controversies. Not all controversy is foolish. Some issues are critical and have to be discussed. But he instructs us to avoid stupid arguments and useless quarrels.

Some of the Jewish rabbis would spend their time building up imaginary genealogies for the people of the Old Testament, and then they'd argue about that. Some of the scribes would spend endless hours discussing what they could do on the Sabbath day and what food they could eat. Some people think they are spiritual if they talk about the Bible a lot or if they argue about it a lot. It's one thing to discuss theology; it's another thing to be kind at home or diligent at work. People can get hung up on the tiny letters of the law and miss the big picture.

Former Governor John Y. Brown suffered a heart attack while he was in Florida. He drove himself to the hospital and told the nurse at the station, "I think I'm having a heart attack."

"Sir, your car is illegally parked," she said. "You're going to have to move it."

He said, "I'm really having chest pains."

She said, "Before you check in, you're going to have to move your car."

"Ma'am," he said, "I'm former Governor John Y. Brown of Kentucky. I think I'm having a heart attack."

"Sir," she said, "move your car and then we'll talk to you."

He went out and moved his car and then checked in.

I understand Phyllis George Brown had some discussion with that hospital after that.

It's easy to get hung up on the letter of the law and miss the big picture. We have to beware of that as a church, too. Some controversies in Christian circles have no solution. They take up endless hours in unproductive effort, and we'd be better off just not getting into them. Some people spend hours and hours discussing premillennial and amillennial views of the return of Jesus Christ. They get into heated debates. People in Sunday-school classes can spend hours and hours talking about whether the world was created in six 24-hour time segments, or whether it was a long span of time in six different segments. Churches get hung up on whether the place they meet should be called the auditorium or the sanctuary; whether the preacher should be called the pastor or the evangelist.

We need to avoid controversy and those kinds of issues for two reasons. Number one, they accomplish nothing. Paul calls them "Unprofitable and useless." When you're finished, often your time is wasted. What virtue is there in having a deep theological discussion that has been rehashed dozens of times when the simple tasks of the Christian life go undone? We get involved with trivia and miss the big picture.

In 1917, when the Russian revolution was rocking the streets of Petrograd, leaders of the Russian Orthodox Church were in a conference just blocks away from the fighting. They were having a heated debate about what color robes the priests should wear. We could spend lots of time on trivia when out there in the world, a revolution is going on. Paul told Titus to spend his time on the real issue and avoid useless, trivial controversies.

A second reason they are to be avoided is that they are potentially divisive. The word for argument here is translated "strife" in other parts of the Scripture. When people get caught up in some of those controversies, they lose perspective. They develop tunnel vision. They begin to get their egos involved. They debate and it results in division. I read years ago of a man who shot and killed another man over a difference of interpretation of the Bible.

Sam Stone wrote, in an editorial in *Christian Standard,* "Some years ago, I talked to a student from a small town where I preached. They had two congregations there, neither running more than 30 people. I asked her how there happened to be a second church in that town. Was it started because of some doctrinal question, or was it because of a personality difference?

"'Oh, it was doctrinal,' she explained quickly. 'The other group believed in having fellowship dinners.'"

It is amazing how people can lose perspective and fight over trivial matters. Paul tells us how we are to handle that kind of foolish controversy: Avoid it, if possible.

One Sunday night at 9:30, my wife and I were leaving the church building with two other couples. It had been a long day and we were exhausted. As we started out the door, my wife said, "Bob, there's a box of pamphlets up in the office. Would you go get it? I need to take them out to Freedom Hall tomorrow morning."

We had guests coming, so I said, "I'll tell you what, let's go ahead and meet our out-of-town guests at the house rather than make them wait, and we'll pick the pamphlets up tomorrow."

She said, "No, we'll forget them tomorrow. Would you go get them?"

I didn't want to make a scene in front of those two couples. It's amazing how in a marriage those little details can sometimes become big irritants. I decided rather than make a scene, I'd go get the box of pamphlets. It's also amazing in a marriage if you've been married a while, you can communicate a lot through an expression. I looked at her with an expression that said, "Now, Honey, I don't want to go get those boxes and I don't appreciate you telling me what to do, but I'm going to do it anyway just to keep peace."

She looked at me with an expression that said, "I don't really care how you feel, go get the box!"

All the way up the steps, I kept thinking, "This is a bigger issue than whether I get the box or not. This is really an issue about who's in charge of this relationship, and I think I need to reestablish my turf." Then I thought, "I'm tired. I don't think I want to get into that controversy tonight."

So I just went and got the box. We went home and had a good evening together because I practiced prevention. I avoided controversy. Because I wimped out, basically!

You can't always wimp out. Some controversies you can't

avoid. Sometimes the issues fester within and need to be confronted. But I think 95% of conflict can be resolved just by avoiding it. There was an old song called, "Fifty Ways to Leave Your Lover." Here are five ways we can avoid controversy.

Number one, *change the subject.* When you feel that a conversation is moving toward controversy, just make a right turn and skillfully get out of it.

Number two, *don't bring it up* if you know it's a volatile subject. You've been over it before. You've battled it before. Don't bring it up again. Fifteen years ago, my parents and I had a heated discussion about divorce and remarriage. We've never fought about that again. I've not brought it up, and they've not brought it up either.

Sometimes, if somebody is forcing the issue, you're better off to just get up and *walk away.* Just walk away from the subject or walk away from the person. Don't fight over it.

Sometimes you can avoid foolish controversy if you *use your sense of humor.* Solomon said, "A cheerful heart is good medicine" (Proverbs 17:22). When Tony Campolo was asked his view on the second coming of Christ, he said, "I don't know. I'm not on the program committee, I'm on the welcoming committee."

You may meet someone who is so primed for argument and so determined that nothing works. The ultimate response is suggested here: "Have nothing to do with him" (v. 10). If you know somebody who is always in the middle of controversy, and they're always fighting about something, *avoid them altogether.* Just say, "Hello. Good to see you. Good-bye." "Bad company corrupts good character" (1 Corinthians 15:33). Some people you just need to avoid.

A grade school boy wrote an essay on "Straight Pins." He said, "Pins are wonderful. They save thousands of lives every year."

The teacher said, "How do they save thousands of lives?"

He said, "By not swallowing them." Prevention is the best cure. Avoid controversy.

## Confront Divisive People
## When Necessary

"Warn a divisive person once, and then warn him a second time. After that, have nothing to do with him" (v. 10).

Romans 12:18 says, "If it is possible, as far as it depends on you, live at peace with everyone," but in Galatians 2:11, the same writer wrote, "When Peter came to Antioch, I opposed him to his face, because he was in the wrong." As much as it is possible, live at peace, but sometimes you have to confront someone to his face. Notice it is the *divisive* person who has to be confronted, somebody who is threatening the harmony of the church—not somebody who disagrees with you, or somebody who's blocking your program.

Three kinds of people can be divisive in the church. First, there is the false teacher. Titus 1:11 spoke of those who were ruining whole households by teaching what they shouldn't teach, and they must be silenced. If a Sunday-school teacher started teaching, "You have to speak in tongues or you're not a Christian," or "When you respond to Christ, it doesn't matter if you're baptized or not," or if someone started teaching, "When you die, you're reincarnated, and we need to practice channeling," then, that teacher would have to be confronted because false teaching is potentially divisive.

A second kind of person who can divide the body is an immoral example. If somebody flagrantly flaunts immoral behavior in the church and refuses to repent, that is potentially divisive. In 1 Corinthians 5, Paul chastised the leaders of Corinth for not confronting a man in their church who was living in incest. He said, "Don't you know that a little yeast works through the whole batch of dough?" (1 Corinthians 5:6) If there's a flagrant immoral situation in the church, the whole church is going to be affected. It could be divisive, it has to be confronted.

The third kind of person who divides the body is more subtle and probably more dangerous—and that is the contentious spirit. Some people have an antagonistic spirit, always stirring up dissension. Maybe it's by gossip. When there are rumors circulating about people, you can trace them back almost always to the same source. Perhaps it's by criticism. They sit back on the sidelines and mumble and ridicule what is going on all the time. Maybe they stir up trouble by anonymous letters. They don't have the courage to confront or the self-confidence to discuss the matter openly, so they write a note without signing their name. Contention can divide by open rebellion. "If you don't do it my way, I'll withdraw my financial support. I'm not going to give my money." It's an attempt at blackmail. Credible leaders never buckle under ultimatums.

Some divide by hypersensitivity. They make it known that they get their feelings hurt easily. People are always walking on eggshells around them. "Aunt Mabel would really be hurt if we dropped the Doxology because her great-grandfather started the church. She probably wouldn't say anything, but her feelings would really be hurt," or "She's sung in the pageant for four years straight. If she's not asked to sing again this year, she would really be hurt." It's amazing the damage done to churches and Sunday-school classes by people who can seem quiet and unassuming, but who hold everyone hostage by the threat of a long-term pout.

This principle applies to the church, but also applies to small groups within the church. One of the blessings of a large church is that it's harder to divide it. It can be divided if the leaders disagree, but in a small church two or three families can create havoc when in a large church they can just be ignored. But these principles apply to small groups like Sunday-school classes, ball teams, and choirs within the big church as well.

If you think somebody is a false teacher, or is living in immorality, or is potentially divisive, you have a responsibility to confront the problem and discuss it with them. If after your discussion, you are still convinced they pose a threat to the harmony of the church, you should have a discussion with the church leaders, and they, then, warn the offender not to divide the body.

Keep in mind that Paul is writing to Titus, who is the

leader of the church. It is not the task of every Christian to confront and warn divisive people. "If someone is caught in a sin, you who are spiritual should restore him gently" (Galatians 6:1). It's a touchy situation. It has to be handled in love.

If there is no repentance, and the body is still threatened, there is to be a second warning. This second warning should be more severe and it should involve more than one leader. Jesus speaks about this same kind of confrontation in Matthew 18:15: "If your brother sins against you, go and show him his fault, just between the two of you." Let's say a young Christian married man begins to flirt with a single woman in your church. You see them together too much. Don't get on the phone and talk to everybody else. If there's a problem, go to that person. If he denies there's a problem and gets angry at you, but the problem persists, what are you going to do? Jesus says, "If he listens to you, you have won your brother over. But if he will not listen, take one or two others along, so that 'every matter may be established by the testimony of two or three witnesses'" (Matthew 18:16). If there's really no problem and you try to get two or three witnesses, people are going to say you're making a big deal out of nothing. But if two or three people agree with you and go to that person and say, "We agree there is a problem," then surely, if his heart is right, he is going to repent.

"If he refuses to listen to them, then tell it to the church" (Matthew 18:17). In a large church, we seldom need to stand up and announce an issue to the whole church. But we say to the group affected, "We think this person has a problem and we want you to urge him to repent."

Then Jesus says, "If he refuses to listen even to the church, treat him as you would a pagan or as a tax collector" (Matthew 18:17b). You speak to pagans, and you are kind to pagans, but you don't treat them as Christian brothers.

That's the same kind of instruction that Paul gave to Titus. He said, "Warn a divisive person once, and then warn him a second time. After that, have nothing to do with him. You may be sure that such a man is warped and sinful; he is self-condemned" (vv. 10, 11). That's an extreme case. If a person refuses to repent of being divisive after a couple of tactful warnings, have nothing to do with him. Withdraw from him.

I can count on both hands the number of times that our elders have gone to an individual and confronted him about divisiveness. I can count on one hand the times they've gone more than once. Usually it's redemptive. We're nervous about exercising any church discipline at all, because ours is an era when everyone wants to be free to live as they please. Secular writers love to expose some of the excesses of the churches of the past. The witch hunts, the burning at the stake, the scarlet letters; now the threat of legal action against us makes us hesitant to practice any kind of confrontation or discipline. But Stuart Briscoe wrote, "If proper discipline is not applied where appropriate, the result will be a marked decline in the spiritual nature of the church."

If you know that the harmony of the church is so important that if you pose a threat to divide it, you will be confronted, you will be less likely to divide. When a doctor takes a knife and cuts into somebody to remove a malignant tumor, that temporarily hurts, but it's for the health of that person. A church leader who cares enough to confront, warn, and practice discipline may cause temporary pain, but the ultimate harmony and purity that results is well worth the discomfort of spiritual surgery.

## Practice Servanthood at Every Opportunity

As you read the final phrases of Titus, you can't help but notice the consideration the early Christians had for each other. "As soon as I send Artemas and Tychicus to you . . ." (v. 12). Paul was sending these two co-workers because Titus was going to leave and Paul wasn't going to leave the church without leadership. He was concerned about the welfare of the church.

Then he said, "Do your best to come to me at Nicopolis because I have decided to winter there" (v. 12). Paul unashamedly expressed his needs and his desires. He said, "I want you to join me for the winter." We can't serve each other if we don't express our needs and confess our faults. I sometimes hear people say, "I was in the hospital, but nobody came to visit me," or "I was home with a bout of depression for a month, and nobody contacted me." Did you tell anybody? If you didn't, how are they supposed to know? "Is any one of you sick? He should call the elders of the church to pray over him" (James 5:14).

Then Titus 3:13 says, "Do everything you can to help Zenas the lawyer and Apollos on their way and see that they have everything they need." These missionaries are going out. They need financial help. Serve them by giving your money. "Our people must learn to devote themselves to doing what is good, in order that they may provide for daily necessities and not live unproductive lives" (v. 14).

The best way to maintain harmony in the church is to get our minds off ourselves and onto serving other people. William Barclay wrote, "Half the trouble that arises in the church concerns rights, privileges, places, and prestige. Someone has not been given his or her place. Someone has not been thanked. Someone has been neglected. Someone has been given a more prominent place on the platform than somebody else and there is trouble." We often think we are fighting for principle when we're just defending our own ego. We're jealous that we're not in the limelight. We're angry because our feelings have been hurt. We look for ways to get even. But when we get our minds off ourselves and onto serving other people, it's amazing how harmony develops. Humility is not thinking less of yourself. Humility is not thinking of yourself at all.

There was bickering in the upper room on the night of the last supper. The disciples were fighting about who was the most important. They were so egotistical, they wouldn't stoop to wash feet. Jesus got a basin of water and a towel. He said, "Now that I, your Lord and Teacher, have washed your feet, you also should wash one another's feet" (John 13:14). There is hardly ever any bickering over the basin.

Jesus said, "The greatest among you will be your servant" (Matthew 23:11). When we start getting our minds on other people, it does marvelous things for harmony. We quit criticizing others. We devote ourselves to doing what is good and we become supportive.

Dan Eynon is 83 and his wife is 81. They are youth group sponsors at a church in Cincinnati. I don't know how effective they are, but they are still willing. You don't hear the Eynons complaining about the youth group in the church. Mrs. Eynon makes a meal for the elderly residents at the Mount Healthy Christian Home once a month. You don't hear them mumbling, "Well, I guess we're getting too old to be appreciated."

Servants are cooperative, supportive people. Jesus said, "As I have loved you, so you ought to love one another" (John 14:34). When we serve one another, harmony is the result. When people serve one another, there is mutual assistance and dependence.

My sons get along much better today. They golf together. They double date together. They wrestle and tease and have a good time. There is one big difference in them. It's called maturity. They are 22 and 18 years of age. Their cooperation and harmony is a real source of satisfaction to me today. While they were growing up, they would often hear their mother say, "Boy, I hope the good fairy came while I was gone." If she left something undone—beds unmade, dishes undone—when we would drive back home and she was tired, she would say, "Oh, I hope the good fairy came and straightened up the house while I was gone."

We left in a hurry the other day and while we were gone, the boys worked together and cleaned up the house. They couldn't wait to hear their mother's comment when we got back. They expected her to praise the good fairy and eventually praise them, but when she got back, she was distracted and didn't even notice. They laughed with each other and said, "Wouldn't you know it? For twenty years, we've been looking for the good fairy, and the one time the good fairy comes, she doesn't even notice."

It is a joy to see a family mature; a joy to see a family laugh and love and serve and work. That's why the Bible says, "Speaking the truth in love, we will in all things grow up unto him who is the Head, that is, Christ. From him, the whole body, joined and held together by every supporting ligament, grows and builds itself up in love, as each part does it work" (Ephesians 4:15, 16).